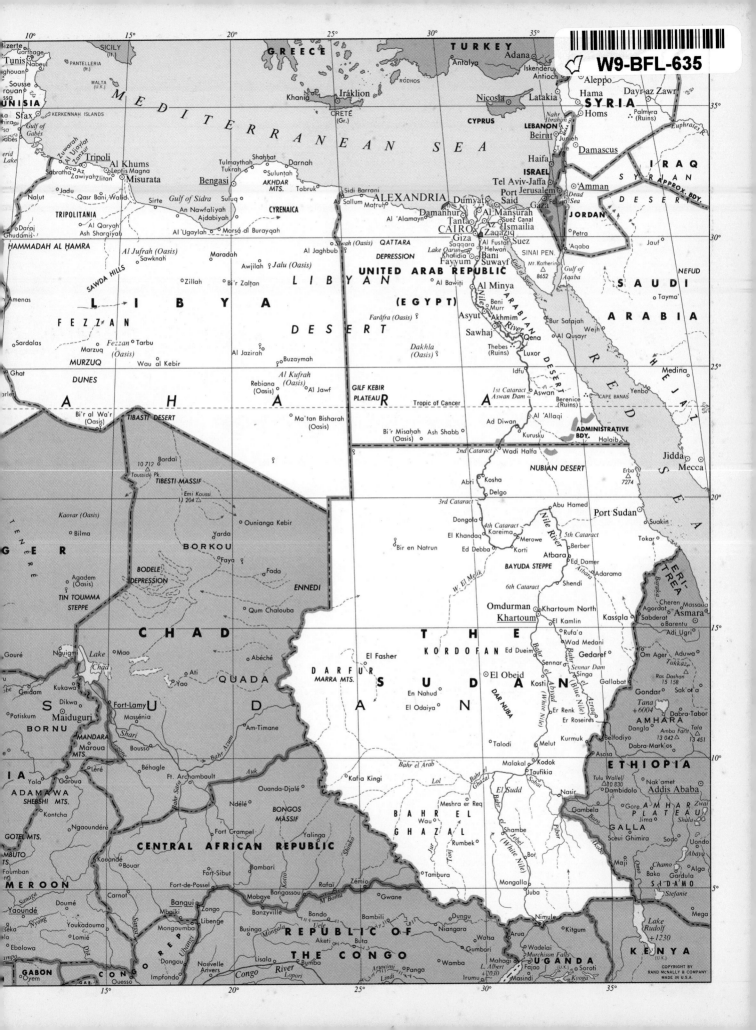

LIFE WORLD LIBRARY

THE ARAB WORLD

OTHER BOOKS BY THE EDITORS OF LIFE:

Life's Picture History of World War II

Life's Picture History of Western Man

The World We Live In
    with Lincoln Barnett

The World's Great Religions

America's Arts and Skills

Picture Cook Book

The Second World War
    with Winston S. Churchill

The Wonders of Life on Earth
    with Lincoln Barnett

Life Pictorial Atlas of the World
    with The Editors of Rand McNally

Life Nature Library

The Epic of Man

The Life Treasury of American Folklore

Life Guide to Paris

LIFE WORLD LIBRARY

THE ARAB WORLD

by Desmond Stewart

and The Editors of LIFE

A STONEHENGE BOOK

TIME INCORPORATED   NEW YORK

COVER: Not far from the life-giving Nile,
the Upper Egypt town of Luxor huddles
in the blazing sun. The town occupies
part of the site of ancient Thebes,
a flourishing city 4,000 years ago.

ABOUT THE WRITER

Desmond Stewart, who wrote the interpretive text for this volume in the
LIFE World Library, is a British writer who has spent many years in the
Middle East. A graduate of Oxford, he taught English literature in Iraq
and Lebanon from 1948 to 1958 and has visited almost every country in the
Arab world. A poet and a translator of Arab literature, he has contributed
articles on Arab affairs to a number of American and British publications.
Mr. Stewart is the author of several novels with Middle East backgrounds,
including *Stranger in Eden* and *The Men of Friday*. He now lives in Cairo.

The Arab World © 1962 by Time Inc. All rights reserved. Published simultaneously in Canada.
Library of Congress catalog card number 62-19070.

Contents

TIME INC. BOOK DIVISION

EDITOR
Norman P. Ross

COPY DIRECTOR   ART DIRECTOR
William Jay Gold   *Edward A. Hamilton*

CHIEF OF RESEARCH
Beatrice T. Dobie

EDITORIAL STAFF FOR "THE ARAB WORLD"

EDITOR, LIFE WORLD LIBRARY	*Oliver E. Allen*
ASSISTANT TO THE EDITOR	*Jay Brennan*
DESIGNER	*Ben Schultz*
CHIEF RESEARCHER	*Grace Brynolson*
RESEARCHERS	*Paula von Haimberger Arno, Irene Ertugrul, Nancy Jones, Renée Pickel, Jean Sulzberger, Helen R. Turvey, Ava Weekes, Linda Wolfe*
PICTURE RESEARCHERS	*Margaret K. Goldsmith, Mary Carr, Sue E. Thalberg*
ART ASSOCIATE	*Robert L. Young*
ART ASSISTANTS	*James D. Smith, Gretchen Cassidy*
COPY STAFF	*Marian Gordon Goldman, Carol Henderson, Dolores Littles*
PUBLISHER	*Jerome S. Hardy*
GENERAL MANAGER	*John A. Watters*

LIFE MAGAZINE

EDITOR   MANAGING EDITOR   PUBLISHER
Edward K. Thompson   *George P. Hunt*   *C. D. Jackson*

The text for the chapters of this book was written by Desmond Stewart, for the picture essays by Walter Karp and David S. Thomson. The following members of LIFE Magazine helped in producing the book: James Burke, Larry Burrows, Eliot Elisofon, Michael Rougier and Howard Sochurek, staff photographers; Keith Wheeler, staff writer; and Doris O'Neil, Chief of the LIFE Picture Library. Valuable assistance was also provided by the following staff members of Time Inc.: Donald Bermingham and George Caturani of the Foreign News Service; Edward Behr of the Paris Bureau; and Content Peckham, Chief of the Bureau of Editorial Reference.

Introduction

Not since the Middle Ages, when its tremendous drive for expansion had a profound effect on the development of European civilization, has the Arab world been an area of such vital concern to the West. Today, as the Arab peoples are stirring once again, both political and economic considerations place them at the center of world attention. Knowledge and perception are necessary as we approach these peoples whose culture is so closely linked with that of the West.

But perception requires mutual understanding. It is fitting that the Editors of LIFE have made this effort to bring the Arab world into perspective for the American reader. I hope the book will also be widely read in the Arab world. As Desmond Stewart's lucid prose and the book's fine pictorial essays bring out, the Arabs are heirs to an extraordinarily rich religious, cultural and scientific tradition whose development in many ways affected that of the West. It was out of the wellspring of the Judaeo-Christian tradition that the Prophet Mohammed brought to fruition in the arid deserts of Arabia the powerful new religion of Islam. It was Arab scholars who first rediscovered the classical writings of Greece, which were later to stimulate a renaissance of thought in Europe. Arab mathematicians, too, formulated systems which the West employs in modified form today.

Despite these cultural affinities, the new and old states of the Arab world harbor considerable feelings of mistrust toward the West, and therefore toward its strongest nation, the United States. Western powers long held undisputed sway over the destinies of the Arab countries; the memory rankles among Arab leaders and citizens alike. Western capital and control long dominated their enterprises; their economies still show the effects. But although the West no longer controls the area, it should not abandon its concern.

The Arab world is an extraordinarily complicated one. Inspired by new leaders, enriched by modern technology, anxious to push forward with an educated younger generation into the 20th Century, it is solving its problems in ways often baffling to western onlookers. For this reason, Mr. Stewart's revealing insight into Arab problems and aspirations should perform a service for international understanding. For without understanding there can be no friends in an uncertain and perilous world.

GEORGE V. ALLEN
*former U.S. Assistant Secretary of State
for Near Eastern and African Affairs*

1

Unity
of the
Disunited

STRETCHING more than 4,000 miles across North Africa and the Middle East, all the way from the Atlantic to the Indian Ocean, a conglomerate of more than a dozen independent nations, protectorates, sheikdoms and other political units is encompassed in a simple phrase: "the Arab world." At first glance, however, that world seems to deny all semblance of unity. Much of it is pure wilderness. One part of this world, the Sudan, is larger than all of western Europe; yet the Sudan has a smaller population than the Netherlands. Saudi Arabia is bigger than Texas and Alaska combined and has fewer people than New York City. Egypt,

the Arab state with the largest population, has less arable land for its 27 millions than West Virginia; more than 95 per cent of Egyptian territory is desert.

A true map of the Arab world would show it as an archipelago: a scattering of fertile islands through a void of sand and sea, islands that stretch from Morocco through the Algerian coastal plain and the thin periphery of Libya to the slim island valley of the Nile, then on to the oases of Syria and Arabia and, finally, the larger island of Iraq. Bahrain and Aden and the oases of Siwa and Dakhla are as minute as Pacific atolls. On this map the desert, like the sea, both

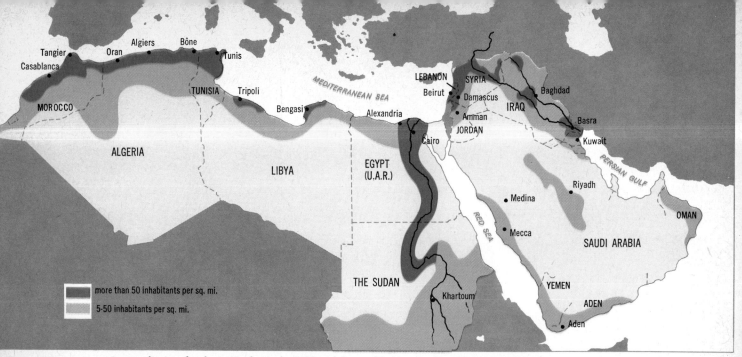

Scattered areas of settlement in the Arab world, each hemmed in by sea or desert, are indicated on a map showing density of population.

divides and joins. On it the small fertile areas outweigh in importance the spaces of *sahara*, the Arab word for desert.

In these oases, large and small, Arab men and women weave the distinctive fabric of their life. New factories are breaking the monopoly of pyramids; new habits clash with old; yet within it all there is a fusion and a unity.

The fabric is visible in multitudinous details. A bearded old man, white turban wound tightly around his red fez, punctures the cold hours before dawn with his age-old cry: "Prayer is better than sleep!" A jet streaks through the pale sky as donkeys patter through village lanes. In government offices and in the bazaars, there is the rattle of spoons in glasses of mint tea. There is the hum of gossip as bolts of vivid cloth are unrolled before dark-eyed women. In coffee shops, the radio, out of tune, blares the news of the day. In curbside stalls boys fan charcoal as meat is grilled. A scent of spice makes an ordinary street mysterious, and when day ends, the night, identified in Arab poetry with the lover, brings magic under the sapphire stars. From the desert, beyond the minarets and palm trees, come the howls of jackals.

Yet, despite the similarity of custom and image throughout the Arab archipelago, it is not custom and image which bring unity to the Arab world. Nor is religion the sole binding force; neighboring Iran, which is as Moslem as the Arab world, is not a part of it, whereas Lebanon, despite being half Christian and half Moslem, is. Rather, the cement which unites the islands of the Arabs is the shared language of Arabic. The fact should not be surprising to Americans who feel more identity with English-speaking nations like Britain than they do with other democratic countries with similar goals and institutions. President Gamal Abdul Nasser of Egypt, perhaps the most important figure of the Arab world, has himself defined an Arab as "anyone whose mother tongue is Arabic."

The archipelago is as disunited politically as it is geographically. The world hears from its newspapers of an Arab League. This League has its headquarters in Cairo. Its members are Morocco, Tunisia, Libya, Egypt, the Sudan, Jordan, Lebanon, Syria, Iraq, Yemen, Saudi Arabia and Kuwait. Ironically, the League was established in 1945 in part because of the promptings of the wartime British foreign secretary, Anthony Eden, who wished to rally the Arabs to support the British cause and who lost his office as prime minister in 1957 as a result of Britain's attack on Egypt in the Suez Canal crisis. The League is too useful for the Arabs to discard; at the same time it is too weak to solve any basic problem. Around one table delegates assemble from states which have not left the Middle Ages and from states which have institutes of nuclear physics. In Arabic, the members of the League render each other graceful compliments. Even when one Arab state quarrels with another, it is with a habitual cliché: "sister Egypt" or "sister Syria," as the case may be. But the quarrels are harsh, and the intrigues are constant. Arab leaders spend fortunes in plotting each other's assassination.

Except on two issues—colonialism and Israel —the Arabs do not speak with one voice. They have a gift for disunion and a gift for uniting against any leader who tries to unite them. Six centuries ago the great Arab historian Ibn Khaldun quoted the Koran, the scriptures of Islam, when speaking of Mohammed's miracle in uniting the Arabs: "If you had expended all the treasures on earth, you would have achieved no unity among them. But God achieved unity among them." This divine miracle, however, took place seven centuries before Ibn Khaldun. Today, despite soothing assurances of brotherhood, it is far harder for the ordinary Arab to move about the Arab world than it is for the ordinary European to move about Europe. There is still no customs union, and mail service between Egypt and Iraq takes several days longer than it does between either of them and London or New York. Currency regulations and the need for exit visas from many states are an additional obstacle. Nor are the Arab countries well-informed about each other. It is rare for an Arab newspaper to maintain a full-time correspondent in another Arab capital.

NO two Arab states have precisely the same form of government. The Arabs are ruled by a miscellany of systems which delight political scientists. There are absolute monarchies like Yemen, where a favorite duty of the all-powerful ruler, the Imam, is watching the public beheading of rebels. Education is minimal, and few foreigners are allowed to travel to this beautiful, backward, mountainous land. Saudi Arabia, Yemen's larger and oil-rich neighbor, has been forced for business reasons to open its doors. But Christians are not allowed in the holy cities of Mecca and Medina, and Jews are allowed nowhere. Those Westerners who live in Saudi Arabia are confined to what can be described only as air-conditioned ghettos. Saudi Arabia is the last country in which slavery is a legal institution. But even "free" Saudi Arabian citizens have no political rights. There are no elections, ministers are largely recruited from the ranks of royal princes and public flogging is the punishment for flouting the Koran's prohibition against drunkenness.

THREE monarchies—those of Jordan, Morocco and Libya—can be imprecisely described as constitutional. In each, inconvenient laws can be suspended if the monarch wishes. The throne of Jordan, a state lacking industry, resources and sufficient agricultural land, was created by the British and is now held in place by money supplied by the United States and Britain and by an army recruited from the Bedouin, or nomadic Arabs, of east Jordan. There are elections, but they are usually rigged. Monarchy has firmer support in Morocco and Libya. Moroccans feel that their king, Hassan II, has inherited some of the *baraka*—a power to confer blessing and fortune—which was held by his father, Mohammed V, whose expulsion by the French in 1953 made him a martyr for Moroccan freedom. In Libya the aged King Idris enjoys similar prestige. A man of simple tastes, Idris is also the leader of the puritan Senussi sect, whose members resisted the Italian occupation before World War II at the risk of torture and death.

The six Arab republics—Lebanon, Syria, the Sudan, Egypt, Tunisia and Iraq—are also dissimilar. Lebanon was the first to be established and is the smallest. It has, in a sense, the freest electoral system. Different parties compete for power, and Beirut, the capital, is served by no fewer than 29 daily newspapers. But the parties represent powerful individuals

11

or religious sects rather than political ideas, and the newspapers are often the mouthpieces of foreign embassies which give them financial subsidies. Thus one newspaper expresses the Egyptian viewpoint, another the French, another the Iraqi, another the British and yet another the Soviet. The Communist party is outlawed, as it is in most other Arab countries, but Communist literature is available.

With four universities (one American, one French, one Egyptian, one Lebanese), Lebanon has the highest level of literacy in the Arab world, around 90 per cent. This achievement is reflected in a political sophistication and tolerance rarely found elsewhere.

Tunisia, another small republic, has much the same pro-western tendency noticeable in Lebanon. But even here President Habib Bourguiba's Neo-Destour party, the group which won independence from France in 1956, behaves as if its opponents were also traitors.

Egypt has been a republic since 1953. The government of President Nasser permits no political opposition, and while the press criticizes individual ministers and individual errors, no general criticism of government policy has appeared in print. Egypt is saved from being a tyranny only because the overwhelming majority of the people back Nasser; they believe that they are in the midst of a revolution akin to war, and they accept consequent limitations on their freedom. The limitations are there, and for those who disagree with Nasser's policies, Egypt seems a police state.

THE SUDAN was given independence in 1956 from what was known as the Anglo-Egyptian Condominium—an administration which was in fact solidly British, with a scattering of minor Egyptian officials. The British bequeathed a democratic system which was technically the purest in the Arab world; the first Sudanese elections, internationally supervised, were honest and fair. Unfortunately the illiteracy (93 per cent) of the electorate and the venality of the elected resulted in a confusion resolved in 1958 by an army coup led by General Ibrahim

Abbud. Since then President Abbud has maintained a moderate military dictatorship.

Iraq is also governed by a military regime. The country has not yet worked out a stable substitute for the unpopular monarchy overthrown in 1958. There is no elected president; elections have been postponed; sovereignty still resides in a three-man council appointed by General Abdul Karim Kassem, leader of the 1958 revolt. The seesaw nature of these new "democracies" is illustrated by the way in which one Iraqi politician—Abdul Salaam Aref —was first of all Kassem's partner in revolution, then sentenced to death for plotting against Kassem, then released. The instability of Iraq, described by Kassem as a "republic of Arabs and Kurds," was underlined in 1961 and 1962 when the government felt it was necessary to shell whole villages of dissident Kurds, the people of the northeastern mountains.

IN physical appearance the Arab peoples differ quite as much as they do in their forms of government. The Lebanese can easily be mistaken for southern Europeans; a certain lushness in their features alone distinguishes them from the more angular Greeks. Their men are hirsute and stocky; their women model Paris clothes with a Parisian flair. It would be hard to imagine a people more unlike the Lebanese than the tall, slim grape-black Sudanese. The greatly varied Moslem Egyptians, the descendants of many races, have intermarried with Arab tribes and Turks. The Christian Copts of the same country retain more of the appearance of the ancient Egyptians, with the same thick lips and swarthy skins. Egyptian peasants are big-boned, slow-moving and massive; their diet keeps them slim, but when they migrate to Cairo they and their women often put on weight. Until recently at least, a big belly was the visible sign of the benediction of God. As against the Egyptians, the Arabs of the desert are thin-boned, glossy-haired and marked by hawklike noses and liquid eyes. This lean fragility may be a transient thing. Better diet in a rich city like Kuwait can in a single generation transform Bedouin into far more robust people.

Yet even the casual western visitor recognizes a unity amidst all this divergence. Whether he alights from his plane in Morocco by the Atlantic Ocean, in Egypt by the Suez Canal or in Qatar by the Persian Gulf, his childhood reading comes back to him. This is the realm of Aladdin and Ali Baba. The people remind him of his illustrated Bible. What he sees is strange, but recognizable.

For however much the divided Arabs modernize, however high they push their skyscrapers in Cairo or Casablanca, however sumptuous the automobiles they drive in Beirut or however gaudy the shirts they put on their backs in the Bahrain oil fields, the Arabs possess a distinctive common culture which they can no more throw off than a hummingbird can change its nesting habits to those of a thrush.

This culture has nothing to do with education. It can be found in university graduates as well as in illiterates. It shows itself in the Arab manner of treating strangers, from an overwhelming social hospitality to a prickly bringing up of political issues. It shows in an unpunctuality carried to the level of an art and in a postponement of plans to the last moment. It shows in the advertisements for Coca-Cola; even in neon, Arabic script is graceful. It shows in the shapes of minarets and mosques. It shows in the trees, above all the date palm under which, according to the Koran, Mary was sitting at the time of the Nativity. It shows in the crowded, secretive alleys of the cities, where the houses gaze inward, and where on the flat roofs both parapets and age-old conventions prevent the men of one household from peering over at the women

of another. It shows in the desert where man sings, noble and alone.

To the Arabs, the identity of their world is reflected in the manners of everyday life, in a way of regarding events—the future, in particular. No one thinks of making a definite appointment; it is qualified by "InshAllah," "if God wills." Nothing is inevitable or fixed; all is subject to a Providence before which men are small. However automatic it may be, reference to the deity is good form. Even atheists (and there are some) invoke the Allah they deny.

Poetry in the past was an Arab bond; at present music, song in particular, takes its place. Um Kalthum, the Egyptian woman singer, is more truly "The Voice of the Arabs" than Ahmed Said, a political commentator for a Cairo radio station of that name. Throughout the entire Arab world, the first Thursday evening of each month is dedicated to her hour-long songs on Radio Cairo; her recitals last long into the night. A woman of around 60, Um Kalthum has the volume of the great Norwegian soprano Kirsten Flagstad, and her popularity is as high with cabdrivers as with cabinet ministers. As she twists her handkerchief between frenzied hands, she wrings the hearts of Arab youth. In Baghdad, lawyers listen to her in their clubs over leaves of lettuce and the potent liquor known as *araq*. In Cairo, it is not necessary to have a radio; Um Kalthum's oceanic voice swirls over the city from other people's.

If the Westerner sees an Arab unity in such external things as the reedy music of quarter tones, the gritty dust that seeps into Arab cities from nearby sands or the shape of the moon over a palm frond, the Arab himself feels at

SPELLING ARABIC WORDS

The transliteration of Arabic words into English is a continuing problem for scholars. Not only does the pronunciation of Arabic vary throughout the Arab world, but several of the 28 letters of the Arabic alphabet represent sounds for which the English language has no exact equivalents. Thus, so common an Arabic name as "Mohammed" has been variously spelled in English as "Muhammad," "Mohamed" and "Mehemet." None of these spellings gives the exact equivalent of the Arab pronunciation. This book uses the spellings most familiar to Americans—for example, "Mohammed," "Moslem" rather than "Muslim," and "Koran" rather than "Al-Qur'an."

home, from Morocco to Kuwait, in innumerable details of attitude. An Arab's king may be at radio war with the next country's president, but when he greets a stranger with *"Salaam aleikum!"*—"Peace be with you!"— he does indeed know the peace which comes from shared assumptions. No one will question him about his wife; he will question no man about his. If he visits a house, he will be told, "This is your home," and if he admires an object, it will be offered to him—and so he takes care not to express his admiration.

The Arab will not offer, or be offered, pork. He will never split a check, in the sense of going Dutch. Whoever pays does so lavishly, for the payer is privileged. The Arab will never criticize anyone to his face, nor expect to be so criticized. When he asks an impossible favor of some bureaucrat, he will not be turned down, but will be given a temporizing answer. Who knows? With God's favor the impossible may become possible. If the Arab visits a friend, he will never be turned away with the phrase, "So and so is not at home," however busy the man he visits may be. Wherever he goes he will be addressed by strangers, even by bus conductors, with some intimate Arabic phrase. He may be greeted as *ya aini* (my eye) or, more commonly, as *ya akhi* (my brother).

THE Arabic language, in fact, is more than the unifying bond of the Arab world; it also shapes and molds that world. Like other languages, it carries within it a whole series of built-in judgments and attitudes. Since it is also the language of the Koran and Mohammed, the Prophet of God, it has an even greater effect on its speakers than other languages have on their speakers. It is impossible for a Westerner to speak Arabic with any fluency without becoming Arabized to a certain extent.

Written Arabic is the same everywhere. When a journalist in Beirut or in Casablanca writes about nuclear tests, he writes in the same language. When an orator broadcasts from Cairo or Baghdad, he speaks in the same tongue, although Egyptians pronounce their president's

first name as "Gamal" and Iraqis say "Jamal."

The journalist and the broadcaster revert deliberately to a formal Arabic idiom as different from the language they use with family and friends as the 14th Century language of the English poet Geoffrey Chaucer differs from modern American—or British—English. This need to switch from the words a man chats in to the words a man writes in imposes a strain on all Arabs. The speaker or writer metaphorically puts on singing robes. He is not quite the same man as the man of everyday. No wonder that what he says on these high occasions often bears little relation to what he really feels.

IF the classical language is the same for all Arabs, the spoken language has differences. These apply to many common terms—good, bad, clothing, health, rain, countryside—but above all they apply to things which the ancient Arabs did not have.

The Arabs of the desert ate squatting on the earth; they did not use tables any more than the Bedouin do today. The ancient Arabs therefore had little need for the word for "table," and modern Arabs use a variety of words for it. An Iraqi puts his chicken and rice on a *mayz;* a Lebanese serves his stuffed vine leaves from a *towleh;* the Egyptian eats his beans in oil from a *tarabayzah.* These borrowed terms are reminders of external influences on the Arab world. Iran is Iraq's eastern neighbor and has given the Iraqis much besides the word for table. Italian influence in the Middle East has given the Lebanese their unit of money, lira, as well as a distortion of *tavola* for table. In Egypt, Greeks long had a near monopoly of small-scale commerce. The Egyptian name for a table comes from a word which in Greek also means a bank.

Whatever the small differences in his language, whatever the disputes of his rulers, whatever the variations in his climate or customs, the ordinary Arab feels at home inside the Arab world. He understands and is understood. To an Arab, every other Arab is his brother, but not always in an idealistic sense. Brothers, after all, have been known to become enemies.

Neatly uniformed Egyptian high school girls file past a bemused street peddler in the port city of Alexandria after a day of classes.

Fruitful Flux in a Once-Static Land

Once mellowed and moldering, the far-flung civilization of the Arabs is being swept today by invigorating winds of change. A fruitful kind of disorder is replacing the old fixed patterns of life. Women in slacks and women in veils, politicians and peasants, oil workers and nomadic herdsmen—such disparate elements march side by side, often conflicting. The old spirit of fatalism is fading as the Arab world senses a renewed opportunity for greatness.

SLEEK HOTEL opened in 1959, the Nile Hilton in Cairo *(above)* looks like a Florida transplantation to the nearby river after which the building is named. The lordly lion stands at the entrance to a bridge across the river.

SUBURBAN TOWERS housing Cairo's prosperous middle class *(opposite)* rise between the western shore of the Nile and the Giza pyramids beyond. The houseboats are a favored abode of artists and theater people.

BLARING BILLBOARD provides a backdrop for a daring young girl on a Cairo playground swing *(below)*. The use of a very un-Egyptian-looking girl in the advertisement is geared to an Egyptian preference for blondes.

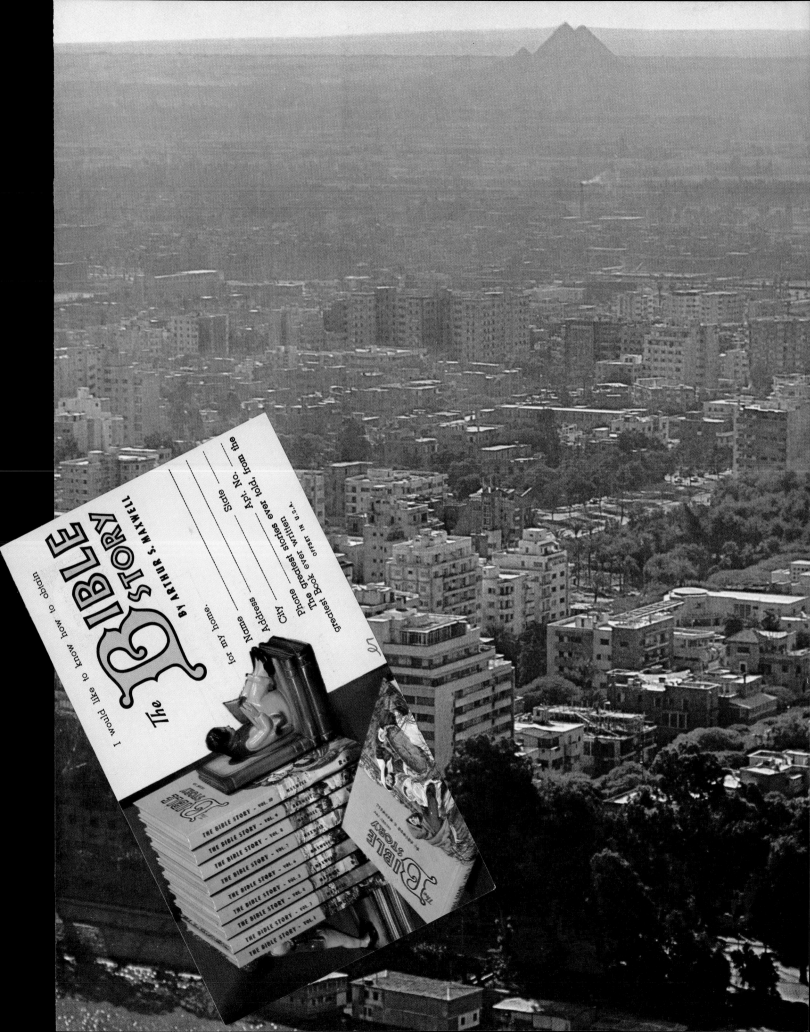

ETCHED BY HISTORY, the Arab landscape preserves the rich markings of

many great conquerors and cultures

WILDERNESS TEMPLE, carved like a giant cameo out of a sheer rock wall at Petra in Jordan, is the work of Romanized Arabs who grew rich preying on passing caravans.

MOTTLED TESTAMENT to Roman power in North Africa, the ruins of Leptis Magna rise on the coast of Libya. The mighty amphitheater was erected around 200 A.D.

A DISTINCTIVE STYLE of building is shared by Arabs of widely differing customs living thousands of miles apart

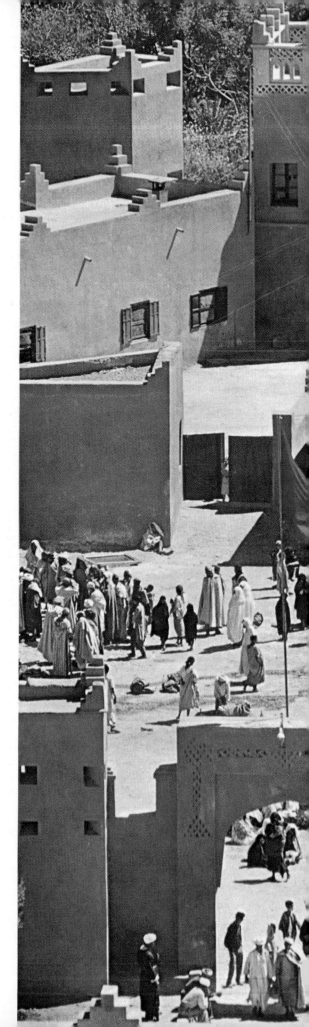

TURRETED PALACE rising skyward above a sunbaked roadside in Aden reflects southern Arabia's long-standing fondness for towering structures.

DOMED SHOP, as cleanly cut as a geometric exercise *(above),* provides a perch for heavily swathed passersby in the Tunisian holy city of Kairouan.

MOORISH FORT, thick-walled yet artfully trimmed *(left),* serves as a United Nations headquarters for distributing food rations to needy Moroccans.

21

On a Cairo street, a trucker sitting behind his donkey looks apprehensively

GOLFING in the infield of a Cairo race course, a sportsman takes a practice swing while his companion watches. Beyond is an observation tower.

ways still blunt the harshness of city life

at a bus speeding past him. Donkey carts are now uncommon in Cairo.

REFURBISHING his merchandise, a tradesman unconcernedly lays out a worn carpet on a busy sidewalk to daub the design with fresh dye.

COMMUTING from midtown Cairo *(above)*, passengers wait patiently to depart. In addition to buses, crowded Cairo has a suburban railway.

A Conquering, Tolerant Faith

FROM the narrow alleys of Algiers on the Mediterranean, from the shadow of oil derricks by the steaming Persian Gulf, men and women prostrate themselves toward one Saudi Arabian town, Mecca. To this same town in its rocky bowl of hills pilgrims have journeyed annually for more than 13 centuries. In the past, they came by camel or dhow or on foot to this unprepossessing place whose summer temperatures tortured the devout; now jet flights and steamers take them to air-conditioned hotels in Mecca's nearby port, Jidda. But the ritual has not changed. Once arrived in Mecca, the pilgrims take off their modern suits or desert robes and wrap themselves in two lengths of seamless white cloth. In the equality of a shared faith, ruler and ruled, rich and poor make seven circuits round a cube-shaped building. Every Moslem wishes at least once in his life to complete this God-centered ritual.

The cube-shaped building, the Kaaba, is covered with black cloth which is traditionally woven each year in Egypt. In the Kaaba's eastern corner is set a black stone. This, Moslems believe, was given to Abraham by the angel Gabriel. The stone is a meteorite, and it has been worn smooth by the millions of lips which have kissed it. Another connection with the times of

Abraham is the holy well of Zamzam, a few yards from the Kaaba. Moslems believe that Sarah's maid, Hagar, found water there when Hagar and her son by Abraham, Ishmael (from whom the Arabs trace descent), were expelled from the tents of Abraham. The Kaaba and Zamzam are now enclosed in a vast unroofed mosque; to the 685 million believers in Islam, the world's youngest major faith, this is the most sacred spot on earth.

Fourteen centuries ago rows of idols stood around the ancient Kaaba. These were overthrown by an impassioned reformer, Mohammed, who was convinced that the greatest sin was to ascribe "partners" to God. Most of the 100 million people who speak Arabic today do so as a result of this man's convictions and this man's words. Both together made an undying imprint on the Arabs and produced what can be called the Arab heritage.

Arabia in the Seventh Century A.D. was as barren as it is today. Except in a few towns on caravan routes, the only living to be made was a poor one. Men were shepherds or camel breeders; there was virtually no agriculture. Those Arabians who had trading contacts with the outside world had some knowledge of Jewish and Christian ideas. Some Arab tribes had thus embraced Judaism, others Christianity. While most of the tribes in the interior remained pagans, they too were beginning to be aware that their paganism gave a less adequate explanation of the purposes of human life than these imported faiths.

MECCA, in which Mohammed was born about 570 A.D., was the richest and most important Arabian town; in its wealth and commercial structure, though not in beauty or art, it resembled the Venetian republic of the Doges. Set in a trough in the mountains of the Hejaz, it lay at the intersection of two great caravan routes: one was the spice route from southern Arabia to Syria, while the other brought the merchandise of Persia across central Arabia to the Nile Valley. Mecca's wealth as a trading center had made it the chief city in Arabia, and its outstanding tribe, the Koraysh, was a leading group in Arabian politics. Mohammed's parents were impoverished members of this clan.

Psychologists might attach importance to the fact that Mohammed, later to be the spokesman of an all-protecting God, was himself born after his earthly father's death and that he lost his mother, Amina, when he was about six years old. His grandfather, Abdul Muttalib, raised him for a further two years, but then he died too, leaving Mohammed almost without a protector in a ruthless commercial society. A Greek historian centuries before had said, "Every Arab is a trader." And it was as a trader that Mohammed first made his mark.

NICKNAMED "the Reliable," the young man of 25 attracted the attention of a rich widow, Khadija, who was 15 years older than he was. She made Mohammed first her business manager and then her husband. He went north, possibly as far as Damascus, with Khadija's caravans; he often retired from the chaos of Arabian tribalism to the desert hills near Mecca to meditate, seeking answers to the problems for which the Meccan idols had no answers.

The answers erupted one day when he was about 40. A voice suddenly commanded him: "Recite in the name of thy Lord!" According to the earliest records, Mohammed's own reaction to this paranormal experience was terror. He rushed home to Khadija. She reassured him; a seer told her that Mohammed had been visited by the same angel who had appeared to Moses and other prophets in the past.

For the next 20 years Mohammed continued to receive revelations—which were to form in their totality the Noble Koran, or Recitation. The Koran was to be for Moslems the supreme miracle, what the Incarnation is to Christians. The early revelations, received while Mohammed was still at Mecca, are both violent and poetic; above all they are exhortations to the Arabs to turn from idolatry and avoid a disaster which otherwise would befall them.

Mohammed's insistence on the oneness and unity of God (Allah, the name the Moslems

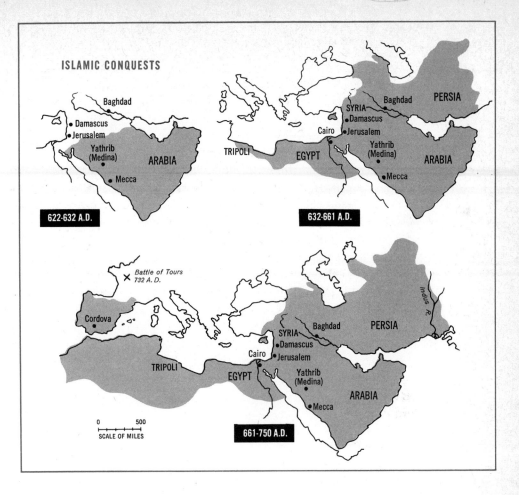

ISLAMIC CONQUESTS

622-632 A.D.

632-661 A.D.

661-750 A.D.

EXPANDING from their heartland in the Arabian peninsula, the followers of Mohammed subjugated vast areas in Africa, Europe and the Middle East in little more than a century, as these maps show. Their surge into western Europe was finally halted in 732, when Moslem troops were turned back at the Battle of Tours by the Frankish forces led by Charles Martel.

applied to the One God, was originally the name of the supreme pagan god) and his consequent attacks on idolatry made him and his followers unpopular with the rulers of Mecca, who had an economic reason for supporting the old paganism, since they derived large revenues from the pilgrim trade to the Kaaba. By the year 622 the persecution had become so intense that Mohammed was forced to lead his disciples into exile. They migrated 220 miles north to a city known as Yathrib, where Mohammed had been invited to arbitrate a tribal dispute. This hegira, or migration, was the start of the Moslem era; Yathrib's name was changed to al Medina, or The City.

At first Mohammed was the prophetic leader of the Moslems in Medina, but as conversions increased, he became the ruler of the whole city. The new religion appealed to the Arabs of Medina not only because it was a system which answered their needs; it was also in Arabic and thus not alien to them. The Arabians had

always been susceptible to the power of words. A later Arab proverb shows their own opinion of themselves: "Wisdom has alighted on three things: the brain of the Franks, the hands of the Chinese and the tongue of the Arabs." The only great art of the Arabs before the coming of Islam was poetry. Annual fairs and carnivals drew poets from all over the Arabian peninsula; the status of a poet was probably higher in Arab society than in any other in history. Mohammed himself warned against the pagan poets, but the rhyming, rhythmic prose in which his revelations were cast and its verbal beauties played no small part in converting the Arabs to his religion. The fact that Mohammed was far from being a literary man, and indeed could scarcely read and write, helped to convince later Arabs that his revelations must have come directly from God.

The new chapters of the Koran revealed at Medina were different in spirit from those that had been revealed at Mecca. They were long and detailed and prosaic, but they showed that Mohammed was one of the greatest legislators known to history. Nearly everything was covered, from inheritance laws to diet. As ruler of Medina, as well as prophet, Mohammed sent polite invitations to the physical rulers of the world to make their "peace with God." (Islam, as Mohammed called his religion, is a noun derived from the Arabic verb *aslama*, which in one form means to make peace, in another to submit; Islam implies the peace of God gained through submission to His will. A Moslem is one who makes such submission.)

Understandably Heraclius, the Byzantine emperor at Constantinople, laughed at Mohammed's preposterous demand; so did Yazdagird, the Persian emperor. Yet within a short time the armies of Heraclius and Yazdagird were overwhelmingly defeated by the inspired armies of Islam. So were the rulers of Mecca. In 630 Mohammed returned to Mecca as conqueror and idol smasher and made the former shrine of Arabian paganism the new center of Islam.

THE speed with which Mohammed's followers conquered Syria, Egypt, Persia, North Africa and Spain—all of which they held less than a century after the Prophet's death in 632—astonished the watching world. The first Moslems who rode out from Arabia felt themselves the bearers of a message of liberation; they were, at the same time, exchanging arid earth for fat pastures and luxuriant crops. To the missionary's quest for virtue was added the pioneer's desire for material gain. Heraclius and Yazdagird had refused the Prophet's invitation to join Islam. Frontier incidents were to the excited warriors of Islam an ample excuse for carrying the struggle into the enemy's camp. Once there, they were to find to their delight that the empires of Byzantium and Persia were cardboard to their steel.

Well led, vigorous and enthusiastic, the Arab fighters were unafraid to die, for they were convinced that death fighting for Islam would propel them into a verdant Paradise. Even more remarkable was the way in which the new faith cemented in unity for action the warring tribes of Arabia itself. Before Mohammed, they had always been disunited. Under his leadership, the surplus population of the Arabian plateaus became the armies which carried all before them.

It was customary once to speak of the spread of Islam as being the work of violence. Mohammed's faith was not pacifist, but its key word was salaam, or peace, and it is certain that its rapid spread was not due only to the skill and courage of its camel-mounted warriors.

For one thing, the Arabs who fanned out of Arabia with the message of Allah and His Prophet were not wholly alien to the people whom they conquered. Just as successive waves of nomads—Greeks, Latins, Celts, Teutons, Slavs—had swept into Europe from the pastoral breeding grounds north of India, so from the heartland of the Arabs, the Arabian peninsula which is edged by sea on three sides and by desert in the north, waves of Semites had migrated in the past to Syria and Mesopotamia. The peoples of the ancient East were largely of kindred stock; most of their languages stemmed from one Semitic source, as does that of the Koran.

Mohammed himself did not claim that he was bringing a new religion. Rather, he said, he was restating an old one. He claimed to be in the same tradition as Moses and Jesus and to be putting the seal on a message essentially the same—for God had revealed Himself through a chain of prophets, "and every nation had a messenger." He taught that Jews and Christians were "people of the Book," and their beliefs were to be respected; at the same time he believed that on certain important points the older religions had gone astray.

THE basic philosophy of Islam was simple. First, the Koran repeats again and again that God is the sole author and ruler of the universe. This concept was not new in Semitic religious thought. Even ancient Egypt, in the 14th Century B.C., had produced a religious revolutionary in the Pharaoh Akhnaton. Akhnaton had rebelled against the official religion with its worship of innumerable gods and attempted to establish a new capital in which one god alone would be worshiped; this god was symbolized by the benevolent sun disk, or Aton, with its descending hands of light. Akhnaton was defeated, and after his death the old idolatry was restored. But Akhnaton's "Hymn to Aton" survives. "Oh thou One God, like whom there is no other," he wrote. "Thou didst create the earth by the heart, thou alone existing."

FROM Akhnaton on, the Middle East produced a continuing chain of servants of the one God through Moses, Amos, Isaiah and Jesus. The Koran makes frequent use of those whom it refers to as the previous prophets, in order to point the lessons which were needed for Mohammed's own people and time.

The simplicity of Mohammed's religion also helped convert to Islam such Christianized peoples as the Egyptians. Earlier, they were ruled by the Byzantine Church and overtaxed by the Byzantine state. Islam offered a simpler faith with few abstruse quarrels over the nature of God, and a simpler tax system. In contrast to the hair-splitting of the Christian theologians, Islam was plainness itself. It required only a few simple beliefs and a few simple actions.

The would-be Moslem had to pronounce the *shahada*, or profession of faith: "I testify that there is no god but God, and Mohammed is the prophet of God." The Moslem conception of God is summed up in one of the brief Meccan chapters of the Koran: "Say: He is God, the One and Only; God, the Eternal, Absolute; He begetteth not, nor is He begotten; and there is none like unto Him."

The acceptance of Mohammed as God's messenger required the convert to accept all the legislation of the Koran as being eternally valid and the Prophet's own life as the supreme example of the right way of living. Thus in addition to praying five times a day, giving alms, fasting during the holy month of Ramadan and making a pilgrimage to Mecca if he could manage it, the convert had to be guided by the sayings and actions of Mohammed. The community ruled by Mohammed in Medina became the

social ideal of the Moslem world. The Prophet lived in a simple house, with the living quarters of his wives around it.

While Khadija was alive, the Prophet was monogamous. After Khadija's death he contracted many marriages, mainly to bind himself by matrimony to the important tribes of Arabia. The wife that he most loved was Ayesha, a girl so young that she brought her dolls to the Prophet's house. To traditions handed down from Ayesha we owe most of the human details that bring Mohammed alive: that, for example, he darned his own clothes, and that the three greatest pleasures of his life were prayer, perfume and the love of women. As a ruler, Mohammed was accessible, humane, decisive and flexible. He could also be severe. When the Jews of Medina were accused of breaking the terms of a treaty between them and the Moslems, he allowed the Jews to appoint their own judge. The judge decreed that the men should be executed and the women and children enslaved, a sentence which Mohammed approved.

THERE was never any separation in Islam between church and state. Mohammed was ruler and prophet at the same time. Islam was essentially a religion of life; Mohammed disliked asceticism, and his rules tended to make life here and now conform to the eternal laws of God. Islam has little of the conflict between perfection and practice known to Christianity. The Koran says: "God has placed on man no burden too heavy to be borne." An observer would perhaps note that the average of Moslem behavior has been higher than that of the Christian. At the same time, Moslem history lacks the peaks of individual virtue achieved by the Christian saints. This is because Mohammed taught a formal pattern of virtue; Christianity encouraged individual acts of heroic sanctity.

Mohammed's last public act was the pilgrimage to Mecca in 632. A few months later he fell ill, probably from the fever endemic in Medina, and died in the arms of Ayesha, leaving no male heirs. His death led to confusion. His followers would not believe that he was dead until Abu

Bakr, his closest friend and father of Ayesha, declared: "If you worship Mohammed, know that he is dead; if you worship God, know that God is living."

Power in the fledgling empire was wielded, in succession, by four of Mohammed's companions: first came Abu Bakr; then Omar, the conqueror of Jerusalem and the ablest general; then Uthman, a wealthy son-in-law of Mohammed, who collected the Koran into one volume; and finally Mohammed's cousin Ali, who married his daughter Fatima, through whose children all the manifold descendants of the Prophet trace their ancestry.

THREE of these successors, or caliphs, were murdered. The fourth, Ali, was assassinated in Iraq and supplanted by Muawiya, a brilliant opportunist who was more interested in establishing an Arab empire than in promoting the religious mission of Islam. Ali's death led to the creation of the one major Moslem sect, since a faction (in Arabic, *shia*) held that the leadership of Islam could pass only through Ali and his descendants through Fatima. Half of Iraq and most of Iran remain Shiite to this day.

Muawiya moved the capital of the Moslem world to Damascus and founded the Umayyad Dynasty, named after his father, which lasted for about a century. For the rest of Arab history, worldly realism and material motives would be intimately entangled with spiritual fervor. But sincere Moslems would always look back to the rule of the first four, or Orthodox, caliphs, as a golden age of Moslem practice. In the 20th Century, reformers and innovators often have justified their new measures by invoking the simple austerity of these early rulers of Islam.

Was the religion of Mohammed democratic or authoritarian? Since Islam is a system, codified and explicitly defined, the question can also be put in the present tense: is Islam today democratic or authoritarian?

It is both. Compared with the brocaded bureaucracy of Byzantium, Islam seemed strikingly democratic. This aspect appealed to the subject peoples of the Byzantines, people like the Copts of Egypt or the Berbers of North Africa who had long been at odds with their rulers. All Moslems were visibly equal before God. They wore the same clothes on pilgrimage; in ordinary life luxury was condemned and in death ostentation was forbidden by the saying of Mohammed: "The best grave is the one you can wipe away with your hand." The first muezzin (the man who recites the Call to Prayer) was a Negro called Bilal. There were no sacraments to be administered by priests. No intermediaries stood, or stand, between man and his God; the man most outstanding for his piety should lead the faithful in prayer.

At the same time Islam was, and is, authoritarian. Allah demands submission and obedience. What is stressed in the Koran is God's majesty, not His love. God issues edicts, not propositions to be argued; these edicts are to be obeyed, not necessarily because they are good, but because they come from God.

Islam accepts social difference. "We have created you in degrees, one above another," says the Koran. The rich man is rich because God wishes him to be rich; the same holds true for the poor; virtue for both consists in accepting their station and living in it according to divine law. Slavery was not outlawed, but the master who freed his slaves was praised. At its best, Islam produces a noble acceptance of fate, something positive and healthy; at its worst, it engenders a passive fatalism.

THE first Moslem conquerors were not fatalistic. Vigorous and enthusiastic, they took with them little luggage but their language and their faith. The early mosques were of utilitarian simplicity, enclosed squares with shaded areas and water available for ablutions.

The Arabs were tolerant conquerors. They rode in Allah's name, yet they did not insist on the conversion of Jews or Christians. These "people of The Book" were allowed to continue practicing their religion with few restrictions; instead of military service (an obligation on all male Moslems) they had to pay a tax. This tolerant approach accounts for the slow but steady spread of Islam and also in part for the attrition of Christian communities like that of the Copts of Egypt. In the Seventh Century the Copts constituted the entire population of Egypt; today they number only about eight per cent of the population.

The Arabs' tolerance extended to culture. They were enthusiastic students of the technical achievements of other peoples. In architecture, for example, they quickly adapted Greek methods of design for their own purposes. The Byzantine rotunda dome was used spectacularly in the Seventh Century Dome of the Rock in Jerusalem. Mosques grew more elaborate; in many cases Christian architects designed mosques for their tolerant overlords.

Even with a Moslem innovation, the minaret, the Arabs were inspired by earlier forms. The oldest surviving minaret, at Kairouan in Tunisia, is a vast, battlemented tower. The most striking was at Samarra, a Moslem capital of Iraq. It recalled the lofty, spiraling edifices called ziggurats which the Moslems found surviving from the ancient cities of Babylonia. This unforgettable shape may well have inspired the design for the first major mosque of Cairo.

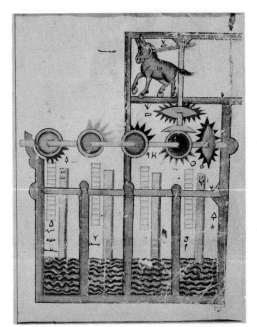

INVENTIVENESS of Arab scientists hundreds of years ago is illustrated by this 14th Century diagram showing a donkey-operated water wheel.

The Mediterranean peoples who were converted to Islam were in many cases technically ahead of the Arabs. Yet the Arabs brought them a contribution of incalculable value. A Greek philosopher had said: "Give me a fulcrum, and I will lift the world." The simple Moslem faith was such a fulcrum. On it a depressed humanity was raised to a new height. Under Arab rule a fusion was worked out between the impassioned monotheism of the Semites and the cultural traditions of the Mediterranean basin. The Arabs became the custodians of Greco-Roman culture at a time when Europe largely ignored that heritage. Unlike many prophets, Mohammed had shown an enthusiasm for learning. A saying of his is often quoted: "Seek knowledge, even in China."

The Arabs obeyed the Prophet and sought knowledge as well as commerce on their great travels across deserts and seas. They developed a practical spirit in vivid contrast with the dogmatism of the enclosed Europe of the Middle Ages. The Arab scholar, whether he worked in physics, astronomy, medicine, mathematics or geography, had far greater freedom of inquiry than did his contemporary in Italy or France. Science, identified in most of Europe with black magic, was the pursuit of innumerable Arab searchers. When Greek science returned to Europe, it did so through Arabic translations.

There were considerable limitations to the borrowings from the Greek tradition. The Arabs were particularly interested in the practical sciences. Their doctors studied and expanded upon the medical treatises of the Greek physician and medical scientist, Galen. Their engineers and architects worked marvels with adaptations of Byzantine architectural forms. Their mathematicians added algebra to the arithmetic and geometry developed by the Greeks. At the same time the Arabs ignored other Greek contributions. These were often the contributions which might have saved them, first from despotism, and second from the consequent inefficiency which eventually laid the way open for their subjugation at the hands of the less humane Turks and Mongols.

Greek drama, with its absorption with moral and political questions, had to wait until the 20th Century to be translated into Arabic. The Arabs seem not to have noticed Athenian democracy and the Greek love of dispute for dispute's sake. The idea that political action could result from popular discussion and a majority decision was not known to the medieval Arabs. The caliphs and sultans had advisers, but an Arabic masterpiece, *Kalila and Dimna*, teaches through fables about jackals and lions how precarious the role of advisers was. Many of the generals and ministers of the caliphs were treacherously murdered by their rulers.

For a brief period in the Ninth Century a school of philosophers called the Mutazilites flourished in Baghdad. Their concern was with theology rather than politics, but their teachings had political implications. They taught, in brief, both that the will was free and that the Koran was not eternal and uncreated, as orthodox Moslems had begun to believe. The ideas of these "free thinkers of Islam," with their free speculation, could have led to political speculations. But the Mutazilites were defeated by orthodoxy, and their writings played little part in the development of Islam.

ISLAM became increasingly rigid. The only outlet for those who sought a warmer and more impassioned religion lay in mysticism. Moslem mystics were called Sufis, and some of them arrived intuitively at a metaphysical position remarkably similar to that of the Christian mystics who flourished later in Spain. One Sufi, Rabia of Basra, achieved a selfless love of God which makes her very close to St. Theresa of Avila. "I have ceased to exist and have passed out of self," she wrote. "I am become one with Him and am altogether His."

But the Sufis had little effect on the direction taken by Arab culture. This culture was Aristotelian, or practical, in everyday affairs, but Platonic, or absolute, in the affairs of state. The caliph was the Commander of the Faithful; his duty was to apply the revealed truth of the Koran supplemented by the Sayings of the Prophet. It is true that Moslem thinkers admitted a democratic source of authority: *ijma*, or consensus of opinion. But this was not to prove a major factor in offsetting the authority of imperial caliph or petty sultan. When rulers were removed, it was by the assassin's knife or the plots of a bodyguard, not by elections.

IT is impossible to understand the Arabs without an understanding of this limitation of their history. The first four caliphs had been as democratic as Britain's William Gladstone, if not America's Thomas Jefferson. In later centuries Moslem potentates were decorative mollusks ruling a harem behind a shell of barracks. Afraid to trust their own people, they imported healthy mercenaries to administer and guard their states. These Mamelukes, or slaves, became arbiters of state, soon learning that the caliph was their tool, and not vice versa.

At its height the Arab empire was vaster and richer than even the Roman had been in its day. It impressed the Crusaders who came to fight it as modern America might impress Papuans. But already forces were under way which would bring its downfall.

The greatest Arab historian, Ibn Khaldun, who lived toward the twilight of Arab power, diagnosed a cyclical process in history, the pendulum swinging between the settled and the nomadic. Civilization was the product of cities. So was corruption. Three generations could sometimes reduce a dynasty from vigor to indolence. New vigor could come only from a destructive outsider.

But there were outsiders whose vigor was to destroy almost beyond repair. In 1258 Mongol soldiers sacked Baghdad, decimating the population of Iraq and ruining the irrigation system. What was left of the once vital Arab civilization, rich in poets and the study of the humanities, was then stitched into the fabric of the Ottoman Empire by Turks whose genius was administrative and military rather than cultural. For many centuries Arabic civilization was to be but a memory—or a dream.

Lofty twin minarets frame the glowing domes of the magnificent old al Ashrafiya mosque built on a lush hillside at Taiz in Yemen.

Glorious Shrines for Simple Prayers

Just as Mecca is the focus of Islam, so the mosque is the center of every village and city. Many are magnificent, some are plain, but all are important in the lives of the faithful. Formal services are held in mosques only on Fridays, but pious Moslems pray there often, and a favorite place to meet friends is in the mosque's arcades. And when the call from the minaret summons the people to prayer, all hearts and minds turn toward the mosque, and to Mecca.

ANCIENT MOSQUES, *some of them*
rivaling in massive simplicity or gorgeous
complexity the great cathedrals of Europe,
testify to Islam's artistic and religious heritage

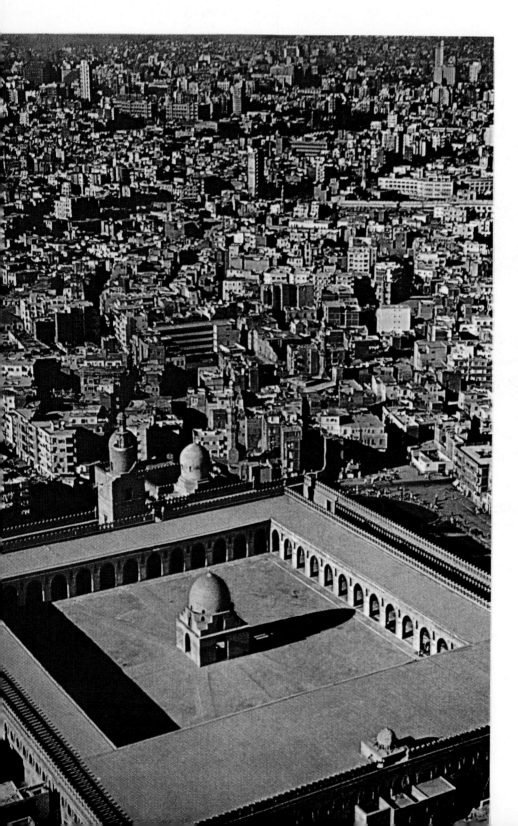

SPIRAL MINARET rises above the walls of the Great Mosque at Samarra. Now largely in ruins, Samarra was once the seat of a caliphate.

FORMAL COURTYARD of the Ibn Tulun mosque forms a symmetrical island in the jumble of crowded Cairo. Its arcades date from 876 A.D.

GLEAMING DOMES and minarets top the intricate, galleried walls of the 16th Century mosque at Kadhimain, a city on the Tigris near Baghdad.

TOUCHING the Kaaba, a cube-shaped stone sanctuary which is the holiest shrine in Mecca, a pilgrim repeats a prayer praising God. Others kneel by the Kaaba's wall and read the Koran.

WALKING around the Kaaba seven times is enjoined on all pilgrims (opposite). The Kaaba itself is shrouded by a heavy black cloth on which the Moslem creed is embroidered in gold.

WAITING to enter the door of the Kaaba (right), pilgrims file past the building that houses the holy well of Zamzam (far right). The pilgrimage takes place every year in the spring.

PERSONAL FAITH, simple in its tenets
and unsupported by any official priesthood, brings
pride and peace to the lives of the pious

PROUD EVIDENCE of a pilgrimage to Mecca is shown by a Moslem who has painted crude pictures of his trip on the outside walls of his house.

FRIENDLY SCHOLARS of the Moslem Shiite sect stroll in a courtyard of their shrine at Najaf, Iraq, while others pray, meditate or even sleep.

BOWING WORSHIPER prays fervently as others pass by in the peaceful gloom of a mosque which stands in the heart of bustling Alexandria.

3

The Perfidy of Colonialism

A TUNISIAN Arab named Habib Bourguiba spent many years struggling against French colonialism. In 1957 he became the president of a Tunisian republic that later sent troops to support United Nations actions in the Congo and whose longtime U.N. delegate, Mongi Slim, won for Tunisia its reputation for moderation in international affairs. Bourguiba, rhetorical and impassioned, showman as well as statesman, has been a complete "political animal" throughout his career.

Bourguiba has told his own life story in articles and letters about politics, in particular in a work entitled *Tunisia and France: Twenty-five*

Years of Struggle for a Free Cooperation. The book's subtitle is significant. Bourguiba spent 10 of those years in French captivity. In 1962 France still occupied the naval base of Bizerte against Tunisian wishes, and 1961 witnessed bloody clashes between ill-armed Tunisian volunteers and the French professional soldiers on the base. Yet Bourguiba—whose first wife was French and whose command of French is excellent— defines his aim as "free cooperation."

The story of European colonialism in Tunisia began in 1881, when French troops landed in the rickety kingdom of the Bey of Tunis and forced the bey to sign the Treaty of Bardo,

41

which made the state a French protectorate. The French had come under the pretext of restoring order and imposing enlightenment. Of later events, Bourguiba wrote: "It was the brutal, implacable taking over by the protector—who had come to 'counsel' and 'suggest'—of all the levers of command in the State. It was the substitution for a protectorate based on treaties and conventions of a regime of direct administration which no longer took the pains to disguise itself. The despoiling of the . . . inhabitants was achieved through decrees."

Later in his book Bourguiba lists his two main enemies: "the bloodsucking colons," or French landowners, and "the vampire functionaries." Tunisia's best land was taken over by settlers from Europe; as late as the 1950s the country's bureaucracy employed more than 10,000 French civil servants.

NOT every Arab country has a leader whose years of struggle have left him with the desire for "free cooperation" with those who ruled. Yet almost every Arab state has undergone the experience of European colonialism.

Techniques of colonialism differed. In Egypt a Moslem khedive (his regal title was upgraded to sultan in 1914 and to full king in 1922) ostensibly ruled, merely "advised" by a British proconsul who wielded the actual power. This resembled the situation in Tunisia, where only a few French extremists envisaged a Tunisia as French as Brittany; there was a powerless bey in his palace, and France claimed to be protecting a separate Tunisian entity. The same was true in Morocco. In Algeria, however, the French tried to digest the whole area and make it an integral part of France. Italian Fascist policy in Libya was similar.

Algeria and Libya thus displayed colonialism in its most extreme form. Algeria's colons (a hodgepodge of immigrants more southern European than French), moreover, did not claim merely to be seizing areas of the North African coast and holding them by right of conquest. Nor did they pretend to be ruling backward peoples for their benefit and eventual self-rule.

The French believed themselves to be the heirs of a superior, Latin civilization which would restore peace to a land ravaged by centuries of strife. Such Frenchmen spoke of "the civilizing French mission," much as the British spoke elsewhere of "the white man's burden." They enforced a cultural, not a racial hegemony; if the Algerians spoke French and assumed French civilization they would be accepted. As late as 1962 Arabic was not generally taught in the French-run Algerian schools.

In Libya, "Italy's fourth shore," the Italians uncovered statues of Roman emperors and also cleared sand from such cities as Leptis Magna and Sabratha. To them their presence in Africa was a revival of an empire they had once owned. They felt that they were *returning* to lands which had once been Roman and Christian and whose character had been temporarily altered by the Arabs. On Rome's Via dell'Impero Mussolini erected a series of marble maps showing the empire of Italy in various periods. His own, which by that time included Ethiopia as well as Libya, was made to appear the vastest of all.

IN one sense the Arab experience of colonialism goes back to the 16th Century. Then the Turks managed to bring much of the Arab domain, part of which had been enfeebled by successive Mongol invasions, into their own empire. The Turkish realm extended from Algeria in the west to the Persian Gulf in the east; of all the Arab lands, only Morocco remained independent. Called the Osmanli, or Ottoman, Empire after its ruling dynasty, the house of Osman, or Uthman, it preserved much of the Arab heritage; but by the 18th Century it was in advanced decay. Militaristic of necessity, it became in its last phase reactionary and opposed to movements of liberation among its subjects. This much can be said without offending modern Turks. Leaders of Turkey after World War I, in particular the soldier-administrator Kemal Ataturk (who took control of the country in 1922 and established the foundations of the modern state), based their reforms on a repudiation of the imperial system. They believed that the maintenance of the empire had been detrimental to the interests of the Turks themselves.

The Ottoman Empire was slothful and corrosive; in its twilight it was also oppressive. In World War I the Turks, like other cornered empire-builders, used torture and the gallows to stifle opposition. But after the war they managed to maintain the independence of Turkey itself against the European powers. The empire's heartland in Asia Minor and a small strip of Europe remained intact.

DESPITE the oppression employed in its final years—applied as much to the Turks of Turkey itself as to the Arabs—the Ottoman Empire had had one great reason to expect a degree of loyalty from its Arab subjects. The empire was Moslem. The Turks had taken their religion from the Arabs; they had also taken their writing and at least 50 per cent of their vocabulary from the Arabs. According to their lights, the Turks were good Moslems. They were not particularly fanatical, as is shown by the refuge they, as well as the Arabs, gave to the Jews expelled from Spain in the 15th Century.

The capital sin of the Turks in the eyes of modern Arabs was that they left the Arabs defenseless against the intrusive power of Europe.

At the time of the Middle Ages the Arabs had been more than the equals of the Europeans (Chapter 2). But while the Europeans progressively advanced from the time of the Renaissance, the Arabs continued to stagnate under Ottoman rule. Rich provinces like Iraq, which according to some estimates had supported 30 million people in the Middle Ages, and Egypt, whose flourishing economy in Roman and Arab times supported at least six million, were underpopulated backwaters, lacking intellectual or political life, with rudimentary educational systems or none, with religion overlain with superstition and medicine replaced by magic. By 1800 Iraq's population had dropped to 1.8 million, Egypt's to 2.5 million. The Turks did not even exploit the potential wealth of their lands, whose economies, in

Iraq's case drastically injured by the Mongols, moldered along with everything else.

The Arabs suffered in other ways as well. In the Middle Ages they had been at the center of the world; if the Europeans wanted the spices of the East or the gold and other products of Africa south of the Sahara, they had to import them through the Arab world. But the discovery of the Cape of Good Hope route to the East dramatically altered matters. The Turkish occupation of Egypt in 1517 had seemed to give the Ottomans a key to the East. In fact, the acquisition brought them little more than the narrow valley of the Nile; Egypt's geographic position no longer mattered.

When Egypt became geographically important again, its importance was to work against the Arabs, not for them. In the 17th and 18th Centuries the European states struggled for tempting prizes in America and India; the Arabs were left to themselves. But at the end of the 18th Century, frustrated in the West by the loss of its 13 American colonies, Britain turned its attention eastward, for the consolidation of its power in India had made the Egyptian bridge between Europe and Asia vital. Since France was the constant rival of Britain, Egypt became important to France too.

The young Napoleon invaded Egypt in 1798; the British caught and defeated his fleet near Alexandria. From that moment the Arab world was never again to lose the attention of Europe.

EGYPT temporarily kept a quasi independence under Mohammed Ali, an adventurer in the service of the Turkish sultan. He massacred the Mamelukes, the descendants of the mercenaries and slaves of the caliph who had taken control of Egypt centuries earlier, and established a dynasty of his own, nominally subject to the Turkish sultan. His descendants were to rule until the abdication in 1952 of his great-great-great-grandson, King Farouk.

Smarting from their losses in the Napoleonic wars, the French invaded Algeria in 1830; they used as excuse the insult given to a French official by the ruler of Algiers (the dey had slapped the Frenchman across the face with his fan).

In 1882, the year after the French had extended their occupation of North Africa to Tunisia, Britain occupied Egypt. Like the French in Tunisia, the British prepared their way in Egypt by an increasing interference in local finances. British and European bankers encouraged Ismail, the imaginative but spendthrift ruling khedive, to borrow from them and to spend on grandiose projects. It was he who on the completion of the Suez Canal invited the French Empress Eugénie to preside over the canal's opening and Giuseppe Verdi to write *Aïda*, with its Egyptian settings, for performance at a new opera house. When Ismail was unable to pay his debts, his son Towfik was appointed khedive. When Egyptian nationalists and their leader, Arabi Pasha, tried to stand up to this virtual puppet of foreign interests, the British moved in.

The successes of the two colonial powers convinced other European countries that the possession of an empire was a major attribute of a self-respecting state. In 1911 the Italians invaded and eventually conquered Libya. Germany had considerable successes in tropical Africa, but in North Africa it was stopped. German intrigues in Morocco were defeated by the French—who thereby established themselves as protectors of yet another Arab country.

In the interim, the British had not been idle. In the late 19th Century they pushed up the Nile under the pretext of reasserting Egyptian sovereignty over the Sudan. After serious reverses at the hands of the Sudanese, they established an Anglo-Egyptian Condominium over the Sudan in 1899.

WORLD'S BUSIEST CANAL

Construction: The Suez Canal was officially started in 1854 when an imaginative French diplomat, Ferdinand de Lesseps, obtained a concession from Egypt authorizing him to form a company to build it. The work, carried out primarily by French engineers and Egyptian laborers, began in 1859 and was completed in 1869 at a cost of $287 million.

Traffic: The canal today transports roughly half of the commerce between Europe and the Far East. As many as 18,000 ships have used the canal in a single year, making it the world's busiest man-made waterway. Its nearest rival is the Panama Canal, through which nearly 11,000 ships have moved in peak years.

Length: The canal is 101 miles long and extends from the Mediterranean to the Gulf of Suez.

The reverses of course had been overcome. The British had overwhelming firepower and the Sudanese little but courage and spears. Yet the reverses were extremely significant. At the turn of the 20th Century, colonialism seemed triumphant everywhere; yet the first counterattacks were already taking place. The Boers in South Africa had been defeated by the British, but only after stubborn resistance. The Indians were beginning the movement which, under Mohandas K. Gandhi, was to gain them independence.

In the Sudan a reformer named Mohammed Ahmed had proclaimed a holy war, raised troops and begun a dramatically successful counterattack against rule by foreigners. His revolt was largely a religious one; he believed that the Sudan's Turkish and Egyptian overlords were lax in their practice of Islam. Calling himself the Mahdi, the "Divinely Guided," he overran a number of garrisons and towns in the Sudan and in 1883 defeated an army of 10,000 men under William Hicks, a British general in Egyptian employ. The Mahdi was not a nationalist leader in the same sense as the Egyptian Arabi Pasha, who in 1882 was exiled to Ceylon for leading a revolt against the pro-British Khedive Towfik. What makes the Mahdi important is that he was able to defy the authority of Egypt, its nominal overlord, Turkey, and the European adventurers they hired to administer the Sudan. In 1885, after a 10-month siege, the Mahdi's forces captured Khartoum, administrative center of the Sudan, despite an epic defense led by General Charles ("Chinese") Gordon, the extraordinary British soldier-diplomat who had earned his nickname by crushing a rebellion against the

Emperor of China two decades earlier. Gordon was beheaded by the Mahdi's troops. This outrage left an emotional legacy which led in part to the eventual dispatch of still another renowned British commander, Sir Horatio Kitchener, to "pacify" the Sudan: the main cause of this expedition was, however, fear of French expansion in the area.

By 1898 the Mahdi movement had been suppressed. Yet the Mahdi and his successor, the khalifa, had for a brief time established a state which lithographed its own books, minted its own coins and made its own laws. The Mahdi's defeat of Gordon and his successor's ability to control, for a period, the destinies of his people were omens of things shortly to come.

IN 1914, when the great powers of Europe clashed, the Turks sided with the Germans. There was some logic in this, for German interest in the Middle East had been commercial, while the British had actually taken over Turkish domains. In addition, Britain and France were allied with Turkey's traditional rival, Russia, and Turkey had been obtaining assistance from Germany for a generation. The Arabs themselves were divided. The religious bond with the Turks inclined some to sympathize with Germany; others felt that the war was a power struggle which barely concerned them. Some Arabs, notably the Hashemite family, who claimed descent from Mohammed and were the hereditary "protectors" of Mecca, firmly committed themselves to the Allied cause. This occurred after the British had given promises to Hussein, the head of the Hashemite clan in Mecca, that most of the Arab areas ruled by Turkey would after the war be granted independence.

But if the Arabs had wanted further proof of the perfidy of colonialism, they now got it. Promises contradictory to those given Hussein had been made elsewhere. After the Russian revolution in 1917, the triumphant Bolsheviks published the secret archives of the overthrown czarist government. The archives included a copy of the 1916 Sykes-Picot agreement between Russia, Britain and France. Under it, the three powers envisaged a postwar Middle East divided among themselves. Russia was to receive areas of Turkey; France and Britain were to split the bulk of the northern Arab provinces of the Turkish empire. Some Arab provinces were to be under direct control; others would be subject solely to the "influence" of the two countries. Only the backward Arabian peninsula was to be allowed to administer itself.

This was not the only contradiction in the promises made by the British. At almost the same time that arrangements were concluded with the European powers and the Hashemites, Zionist leaders in London were being informed, as the declaration issued by the British foreign minister Arthur Balfour put it in 1917, that His Majesty's Government looked "with favor" on the "establishment in Palestine of a national home for the Jewish people." In 1917 the population of Palestine was more than 90 per cent Arab; Balfour himself seems to have attached little importance to this fact.

It is true that the mandates finally issued to the European powers by the League of Nations were envisaged as ways of preparing the inhabitants for self-government; it is true that the Balfour Declaration was hedged around with provisos that the interests of the Arabs were to be safeguarded. But the nationalists in Egypt, whose advice all along had been to trust neither the Allies nor the Turks, were proved right.

After the publication of the Sykes-Picot agreement and the issuing of the Balfour Declaration, trust between the Arabs and the Allies was undermined. In the interwar years, those who worked with either British or French officialdom were increasingly regarded as traitors.

YET many Arabs did continue to work with the Allies—the Hashemites in particular. This family had more pretensions than skill, however. Supreme in Mecca and its surrounding areas alone, it soon lost that supremacy to the far more capable and determined warrior Ibn Saud, whose tribe had been important in central Arabia since the 18th Century. Saud and his forces chased the Hashemites from Mecca in 1924-1925 and united most of Arabia under his rule, eventually naming it Saudi Arabia.

The expelled Hashemites were now dispossessed noblemen. But instead of turning into Paris cabdrivers, they continued to collaborate with the British, ignoring the contradictions in British promises in order to hold what could be held. Two of King Hussein's sons—Feisal and Abdullah—had thrones made for them by the British. Feisal, driven out of Syria by the French, was established on the throne of Iraq, while Abdullah was made emir of the newly created principality of Transjordan.

All these actions reinforced the Arabs' basic mistrust of the imperialists—a mistrust which was eventually to cost the Europeans their Arabian holdings. Despite the extent and apparent stability of colonialism, its time was finished. The European powers had managed to gain the northern coast of Africa and much of the Arab East in a century; shortly after World War I they were in control of almost the entire Arab world. But within a generation the colonial territories were to disappear and colonialism was to be a memory—or a scar.

To speak of colonialism in moral terms leads to heated blood. Those who defend it argue that the colonized are ungrateful for benefits bestowed; those who oppose it become apoplectic at memories of insult and despoliation.

IT is best to examine the colonial epoch not only objectively but nonmorally. For colonialism can best be understood as a fact of nature, a major collision between the Arab world and a fast-developing, arrogant and technically superior European civilization. The collision was painful, but it was also rewarding. In the past the Arabs themselves had collided in much the same way with less-developed peoples, although the fact is something they are inclined to forget. Arab traders (and slave traders) had penetrated south of the Sahara; their arrival had brought a more sophisticated religion to much of tropical Africa, and it is notable that the religion of the Arabs is still spreading far more successfully in Africa than Christianity.

If we approach colonialism as a nonmoral fact, we can note certain things of value that it brought. Napoleon invaded Egypt for selfish reasons. But he brought with him some of the idealism of the French Revolution. From the collision with its ideals Egypt has never recovered, nor wished to recover. Throughout the 19th Century Egypt had the richest intellectual life of any Arab state, with fervid translating from European languages and a fusion between traditional and modern ideas which was not found elsewhere. Napoleon shelled Cairo from the Mokattam hills east of the city, but he also opened the country to the world.

IRAQ, on the other hand, slumbered throughout the 19th Century as the most dismal of Ottoman provinces, with scarcely a secondary school and little intellectual or political life. This heritage shows in a certain lack of maturity in modern Iraq. Nevertheless, the British mandate imposed on Iraq after World War I brought positive benefits. The civil service was modernized, schools were opened, finances were put in order and the oil industry was started.

Every other Arab state which has been under foreign control owes some debt to its master. The Sudan was under joint control of Britain and Egypt. The administration modernized the country's legal system, built railroads and suppressed the slave trade.

Libya under the Italians began to grow food on a large scale for the first time in centuries; the agricultural economy established by the Romans, weakened by constant fighting and tribal raiding over the centuries, had been finally destroyed by ferocious Bedouin nomads in the 11th Century. Under Ottoman rule the major occupations of the scant population had been piracy and the slave trade. The Italians reclaimed thousands of acres for agriculture.

In Algeria, too, which in previous centuries had produced little except pirates, agriculture was developed. The fact that the Algerian Arab population increased almost fourfold in a century testifies that the French brought at least some benefits to the country.

To sum up what may be said in favor of what every Arab radio station denounces as *isti' mar*, a word which is translated into English either as "colonialism" or "imperialism" but which derives from a verb meaning "to inhabit": the Arab countries which collided with Europe have today more progressive societies, in every case, than those Arab countries—like Saudi Arabia, Yemen and some sheikdoms of the Persian Gulf—which were not directly administered by the colonial powers.

But if the colonizers brought good, this was, as an Egyptian reporter once said, as the bird of prey brings seeds—stuck by accident to its claws. For colonialism was to its victims (or to its beneficiaries) a traumatic experience.

The world is inclined to regard Jews and Arabs as opposites, like cops and robbers. In fact they share, besides a Semitic origin, a similar historical wound. For what the ghetto and the concentration camp were to the Jews of Europe, the foreign occupation of their countries was to the Arabs.

No modern Arab will pause in conversation to pay tribute to the benefits brought by colonialism, unless he is alone with his companion and remarkably broadminded. What oppresses the Arabs is the memory of exploitation and insult at the hands of their occupiers.

THE exploitation and the insults differed. In Libya, as in Algeria, there was an attempt to destroy Arab culture. When the Arabs refused to accept the authority of their overlords, they were massacred. Stories are still told in the Arab world that the Fascists dropped Arab resistance leaders from airplanes in the Libyan province of Cyrenaica. The Italians were gentler in the province of Tripolitania. As a result, there are Tripolitanian Italians working alongside Arabs in Libya today, while all the former settlers have left Cyrenaica.

In Egypt, the British "advised and counseled," but their control was complete. Under British influence, Egypt was preserved as a cotton farm for the mills of Lancashire, the British textile center. Egyptian industrialization—the

only solution for the problems presented by a rapidly increasing population—was deliberately blocked. The British supported the conservative monarchy, and Egyptian reformers were balked by the alliance.

Similar indirect techniques were used in Iraq. After 1932 Iraq was independent; the British were nominally allies, not overlords, although an Iraqi-British treaty gave the British ambassador precedence over other diplomats. The ruling Hashemites were, however, dependent on British support, and most of them did what they were told. The throne, the parliament and the large landowners were allies. In 1941, when Britain was struggling for survival against the Nazis, the Iraqis under Premier Rashid Ali al Gailani revolted and briefly joined the Axis. The action was taken not out of sympathy for Nazism, but in obedience to the maxim that an enemy's difficulties are one's opportunities.

THE British crushed the wartime revolt in a month, and their end in Iraq was not to come until 1958, when the last of the Hashemites was overthrown. So bitter were Iraqi feelings against the British that for a while in 1959 there seemed a danger that the country would swing to Communism. The British by now had lost power and learned sense. They did not try to restore the Hashemites, and thus probably saved Iraq for the West.

But the commonest and angriest reproach on Arab lips is not any particular atrocity in one of the occupied Arab countries, but the loss of what they still refer to as Palestine. There is no racism involved in the Arab attitude toward Israel, as indeed there hardly could be, since the Arabs are themselves Semites.

The Arab attitude toward Palestine is simpler. Until 1917 Palestine was an Arab country in which the small Christian and Jewish minorities lived in harmony with the 90 per cent Moslem majority. To Moslems, as well as to Christians and Jews, Palestine was a holy land: from Jerusalem, according to tradition, Mohammed was mystically conveyed to heaven. Nor was Palestine backward before the establishment of Israel; under the British Mandate it had become a country in which the Arabs had reached a high level of education and productivity.

After the Balfour Declaration, the character of Palestine began to change. Just as the Italians had begun the settlement of Libya, exporting hundreds, then thousands, then tens of thousands of Italians to build villages on what had been Arab land, so in Palestine the Zionist colonists—backed by what seemed to be a formidable international machinery and unlimited money—began to build villages and farms at strategic points throughout the country.

Of course the British continued to promise that nothing would happen which could harm Arab interests, and some of the Jewish settlers genuinely wished to live in amity and equality with their neighbors. But by the late 1930s the Arabs no longer trusted soft words from Europeans, and to them the Jews were Europeans. They had heard noble sentiments from the French in Algeria, they had heard promises repeated *ad nauseam* from the British that Egypt would be evacuated. Yet in Algeria and Tunisia, Arabs were not welcome in European cafés and some European towns. In Egypt the British army went where it wished; Egyptians believed that cabinet changes were decided at the British Embassy.

THE parallel with Libya is worth repeating. For in Libya the Italians discovered relics of their ancestors. Headless statues of the imperial Caesars were floodlit in marble niches as evidence of the Italian right to "return" to this Arab country. So in Palestine, the Jews claimed the right of "return" to the Canaan of history. In both cases, the Arab opposition was based on the belief that no foreigners from Europe had the right to use ancient history or mythology as a pretext for dispossessing them from their own lands.

Thus in Palestine occurred a clash between two wounded peoples, each obsessed with its own case, each unaware of the intensity of feeling aroused in its opponent. Most Arabs had little comprehension of the sufferings of Jewry, though a number of Jewish refugees had found sanctuary from Hitler in Cairo and Baghdad. Those who understood the measure of Jewish suffering in Europe would have argued: "We have always treated the Jews fairly. Let those who have persecuted them make atonement—in their territory, not ours." But the Jews saw Palestine as an immediate refuge. The rights of the Arabs who already lived in Palestine seemed less immediate than their own needs.

THUS in the 1960s the Arab world was almost entirely decolonized; yet to Arabs everywhere the most flagrant example of colonialism remained Israel—a wedge neatly dividing half of the Arab world from the other.

To the Israelis, Israel became a fulfillment of prophecy. To non-Jews with a consciousness of guilt, it may represent a measure of atonement for anti-Semitism, whose modern manifestations outdo the wrongs inflicted on Jews by the Spanish Inquisition or upon Christians by the Roman emperors. To all the Arabs, however—not just the million-odd Palestinians who once farmed or traded in the fertile plain between Gaza and Lebanon—Israel is simply the cunningest fulfillment of imperialism, the incarnation of "divide and rule," the constant reminder of colonial menace.

In Arab eyes, Israel's drive into Egypt's Sinai peninsula in 1956, followed by the Anglo-French attack on the Canal Zone during the Suez crisis, only proved what they had long believed: that an expansionist Israel was also a springboard for imperialism. Western enthusiasts for Israel's progress and/or military prowess remind the Arabs of those who in the past have argued for colonialism. In the 1930s, some Westerners applauded Mussolini's efforts to establish an African empire, and Arabs recall that as late as the early 1960s Frenchmen in Algiers tooted auto horns to a rhythmic slogan that showed their wish to keep Algeria French: *"Al-gé-rie Fran-çaise!"* That Israel was strong only made Arabs the more afraid of it; that it was westernized only made it seem more alien.

Led by Britain's T. E. Lawrence (mounted near the banners), Bedouin raiders form for battle during the Arab revolt of World War I.

The Turbulent Demise of Imperialism

At the end of World War I, virtually every lever of power in the Arab world was operated by a European nation. British officers commanded Arab troops, and French bureaucrats bolstered puppet pashas. Some of the very nations which today constitute the Arab world were created at European peace conferences. In Iraq and Jordan, three generations of Hashemite kings owed their authority to British support which began during wartime *(above)*. Today, except in scattered parts of southern Arabia, the imperial purple is being driven violently from the scene. Europe, with its economies lubricated by Middle Eastern oil, still keeps its hand in the Arab world. But many of the European-backed rulers have been discredited, or assassinated. Nationalism now pulsates through the Arab world. More and more, Arabs who speak for Arab independence and Arab prosperity are the ones who are manipulating the levers of power.

JORDAN, dominated for years by Britain, leads a perilous existence under a young monarch

IMPERIAL LINK between Jordan and Britain *(right)*, John Bagot Glubb, English head of the Arab Legion, tours a military post with former King Abdullah. The king was put in power by the British because his family aided them in World War I. The Legion was financed for years by Britain to bolster the pro-British monarchy.

BRITISH PROTEGE, former King Abdullah *(opposite)* visits the Dome of the Rock, famed Islamic shrine in the Arab section of Jerusalem, during the 1948 Arab-Israeli hostilities. Because Abdullah negotiated with Israel at that time, he was bitterly denounced by many Arabs as a traitor. He was assassinated by an extremist in 1951.

LONE SURVIVOR among the British-backed Hashemite monarchs is young Hussein *(center)* of Jordan. With his pro-British heritage, Hussein is disliked by the radicals sympathetic to Egypt's Nasser. To show his independence of Britain, Hussein in 1956 relieved Glubb of his command and has since tried to steer his own course.

IRAQ, having overthrown its pro-British monarchy, is now ruled by a dictator

ILL-FATED DYNAST, King Feisal II sits glumly on a throne controlled by his suave, Anglicized uncle, Emir Abdul Ilah *(center)*. Both were slain in the 1958 revolt.

LOOTED PALACE is examined by rebel leaders after a Baghdad mob swarmed over it with sticks and knives on the bloody day when King Feisal was murdered.

REVOLUTIONARY JUSTICE is meted out to Feisal's secret police chief in the "People's Court," where a lust for revenge ran wild in the days following the revolt.

REBEL CHIEF, General Abdul Karim Kassem is congratulated on the quick success of the soldier-led rebellion. His regime has become an insecure military dictatorship.

PRIZED WATERWAY, the Suez Canal is entered from the Mediterranean Sea *(above)* at Port Said. For 87 years the canal was operated by the Suez Canal Company, a corporation controlled mainly by British and French interests. In 1956, President Nasser precipitated a grave international crisis by seizing control of it for Egypt.

THE SUEZ CRISIS proved that

a foreign show of force could

no longer sway a strong Arab regime

ANGLO-FRENCH ATTACK on Port Said *(above)* in 1956 was an attempt to challenge Nasser's takeover of the canal. The attempt failed, and the canal remained Egypt's.

NATIONALISTIC ZEAL during the crisis spurs Egyptians *(right)* to topple the statue of Ferdinand de Lesseps, the Frenchman who directed the canal's building.

THE WOUNDS of war and political turmoil remain unhealed, creating tragic problems that have long defied solution

UNEASY SOLDIERS of the French army *(left)* stand guard over a battered street in Algiers during a big general strike joined by Moslem merchants who closed down many of the Casbah's shops. Arab independence is drawing nearer in Algeria, but only after a war that has cost the lives of some 250,000 Arabs and Frenchmen.

TROUBLED REFUGEES wait for food at a camp in the Gaza Strip *(opposite)*. The refugees, in their camps near the Israeli border, are mainly Arabs who fled Palestine in 1948 when the Jews won control of the area. More than a million of them now exist in a political limbo and are largely supported by United Nations relief.

At a Levantine-style party given by a millionaire Arab businessman, a Lebanese dancer named Kawakib performs the traditional

A Society
between
Two Poles

belly dance. As Kawakib danced, the guests clapped and sang.

THE Arabs live and die between two seas:
the secret, inner sea of the desert, and the
open, communicating Mediterranean. The earliest Arab cities, such as al Fustat in Egypt just
south of modern Cairo, or Kairouan in Tunisia, hugged the desert, not the sea. In the desert
the Arabs felt secure since they and no one else
knew the water wells and the safe routes across
the shifting sands. Not even the imperial Roman legions had been able to conquer the men
who knew the desert. But as Arabs settled along
the coasts of the Mediterranean, they absorbed
important elements of the culture of the Greeks
and Romans.

Throughout their history, down to the present day, these two seas have occupied opposite
poles in the consciousness of the Arabs. Every
Arab may be said to have one soul which looks
outward to the sea and another which looks
inward to the desert. In some Arabs one pole
dominates to the exclusion of the other. The
two poles may be called the Levantine and the

Zealot. Both extremes are often reactions to the impact of the West, which has seemed aggressive, successful and infinitely rich to most Arabs. The Levantine is drawn to this external force; the Zealot reacts against it.

Levantine is an old-fashioned word. In Italian *levante* simply means the east, the part of the world where the sun rises. To the Italians this means the shores of the eastern Mediterranean. But the word long ago came to be used to describe the people who lived between the Mediterranean coasts of Turkey and those of northern Egypt. Levantine was never a precise term, and it was hardly ever a compliment. It referred usually to non-Moslem dwellers in the Arab world, and in particular to Greeks unsettled from Greece, Armenians in exile from Armenia, and a miscellany of surviving Christians or Jews in whose hands reposed the commerce of the area. It could apply by extension to those Moslems who adopted such ways of living and behavior. The Levantine of myth—and often of fact—was smooth, perfumed, elegant and inclined to stoutness. While he sometimes wore the red conical hat known as a tarboosh, he kept his loyalties with whatever bank in London or Paris kept his cash. He was often extremely intelligent—which may have been one reason why he was unpopular with the brawny Anglo-Saxons who bore with athletic insensitivity "the white man's burden."

THE high-water mark for Levantine success was the period when European powers controlled the Arab world. Levantines were among the richest men in the world. One such was Calouste Gulbenkian, the Armenian millionaire who acquired a five per cent interest in the Iraq Petroleum Company. Gulbenkian loved art and preferred money and solitude to people. Other Levantines have created art, not merely acquired it. The Lebanese Georges Schéhadé, author of the 1957 play *L'Histoire de Vasco,* is considered an important French writer. The late Constantine Cavafy of Alexandria was among the best modern poets anywhere. Living in a prosaic city (unlike the shimmering metropolis described in the best-selling novels of Lawrence Durrell), he transfigured the Levantine present with the glow of the Greek past: "To the great honors of our race my thoughts return, / The glory of our Byzantine achievement."

Speaking of a youth wounded in a brawl, Cavafy writes: "Medes, Syrians, Greeks, Armenians, we're a mixed pack. / Remon is that sort too. But when shining / We saw his countenance yesterday in the moonlight, / Our thoughts to Plato's Charmides went back."

Few Levantines go back, either in thought or race, to Plato; many live in a commercial present of money-making and intrigue. Yet the Levantine artist or businessman can be a man who has honestly decided that the West—whether arrayed in the guise of America, England or France—has more to offer him than his own world. The decision may not be heroic, but it may be wise. No one rebukes the Polish-born Joseph Conrad for writing his novels in English rather than Polish.

THE geographic and spiritual center of the Levant is Lebanon. This nation is a natural island in the featureless plains of the Middle East. Half the size of neighboring Israel, Lebanon enfolds a startling variety of scene within its coastal plain, its two ranges of mountains and its Bekaa Valley. Ancient Lebanon was a pagan holy land: its chief shrines were associated with Adonis, the shepherd who was loved by Venus and slaughtered by a boar near the source of the Lebanese river Ibrahim. The Phoenicians who then inhabited Lebanon were Semites—who lacked the obsession with righteousness of the Hebrews or Arabs. Yet their contributions to civilization were great. To serve their commercial interests, the Phoenicians developed around 1700 B.C. the first truly phonetic alphabet. From it all modern alphabets derive. From little harbors in Tyre and Sidon their ships ranged across the Mediterranean and out into the Atlantic. Phoenician merchants reached as far as Cornwall on the southwestern tip of England, and Phoenician objects have been found all along the western bulge of Africa. They were great colonists; Queen Dido of Carthage, the state which once fought Rome for mastery of the Mediterranean world, is supposed to have come from Tyre.

Lebanon was early converted to Christianity; Jesus had Himself visited Tyre and Sidon, and legend connects Mary with Harisa, a shrine 15 miles north of Beirut. When the Arabs swept through the Middle East and converted most of it to Islam, Lebanon remained largely Christian. The dominant sect became the Maronite Church, named for its Fourth Century patron saint, Maron. For many centuries the mauve and white mountains of Lebanon were a refuge for Middle Eastern Christians made uneasy by the Moslem majority. Their sense of being an island of Christianity in the Islamic sea gave the Lebanese mountaineers energy as well as a pro-western impetus.

In the 17th Century, close contacts had been established between the French and the Maronites. The Maronites wanted support against the Ottoman Turks, and the French saw in Lebanon an opening for trade with the Levant. By the mid-19th Century the Lebanese had managed to achieve a form of local autonomy within the Ottoman Empire. American as well as French influence began to appear in Lebanon. In 1866 American missionaries established the Syrian Protestant College in Beirut, so called because at that time the area known as Syria included what are now Lebanon, Syria, Jordan and Israel. The Syrian Protestant College was later to grow into the American University of Beirut. The printing presses of Beirut played a major role in awakening Arab consciousness against the Turks, though the motive of many Lebanese was more to counter the Turks than to support Pan-Arabism.

DURING World War I the dying Turkish empire lashed out against the Arab nationalists of the area, hanging patriots in Lebanon and in neighboring Syria who had been conspiring to end Ottoman rule. After the war Syria and Lebanon were placed under French mandate. The Arabs, who had been promised independence by the western powers, felt betrayed. But the Christians in Lebanon, who believed that they would be better off under the rule of the Christian French, were less restive. French planes and guns had to bombard the peoples of Syria into silence, but the Lebanese stayed comparatively quiet, absorbing French culture and laying the basis of an overseas financial empire. Eventually, in 1946, the Lebanese achieved the independence promised them early in World War II by Free French forces wishing to counter increasing German influence in the area. Earlier, the French had extended Lebanon's frontiers. In the process, they had also greatly enlarged its problems, since the expanded country now contained as many Moslems as Christians.

THE Lebanese are the greatest travelers in the Arab world. As with Scotsmen, there are more of them outside their country than inside. Their largest colonies are in North and South America, but the Lebanese are present in considerable numbers in West Africa and in Manchester, England, where they play a role in the cotton trade. There are also Lebanese colonies in other countries of the Arab world. The most important is in Egypt, where the Lebanese did much to start the Egyptian motion-picture and newspaper industries.

Beirut, the capital of Lebanon, plays a more important role than its population of 500,000 would indicate. Cosmopolitan and easygoing, it has fewer restrictions than any other Arab city. As well as producing fruit and wine, Lebanon has developed some light industry, but the Lebanese are aware that their prosperity depends on their being an open door to anyone who wishes to come in. Restaurants, brothels, gambling casinos and money changers are more the symbols of Lebanon than the cedar tree which is the country's emblem. Although at least half of the population is Moslem, the impress to the society is given by the Lebanese Christians. It is they who import the latest from the West, whether air conditioning or the newest dance craze. Convention requires that the president of Lebanon be a Maronite Christian and the premier a Moslem; the former holds the more important office.

It is easy for the foreigner to satirize the Lebanese as they indulge in a particular Levantine pastime—that of talking in two or even three languages all at once. But it is wiser to see Lebanon for what it is, an invaluable element in the Arab world, a port of entry for modern ideas and techniques. One of the new Lebanese is Emile Bustani, a self-made millionaire who employs 14,000 workers on building and trading enterprises throughout the Middle East and Africa.

A tycoon of American dimensions, Bustani is not simply a businessman: he is also a connoisseur of good wines, a published author and, more significantly, an Arab nationalist. Bustani would like his city, Beirut, to symbolize more than easy sex and easy dollars. He is the president of the American University of Beirut Alumni Association, and in an area whose rich men have rarely been philanthropists he is known for his generous donations to worthy causes. There is a continuing need in the awakening Arab world for men of Bustani's dynamic, even impudent, energy.

But men like Bustani are still exceptions in the Levantine world. Far more common are the noncreative middlemen whose fingers simply pick off a percentage on goods made by others and whose only *patrie* is their pocketbook. Such are the Levantines of legend, and still to some degree of fact: men who see western civilization in terms not of applied energy and free inquiry, but of material comfort. This type of

THE LEVANTINE'S LANDSCAPE

Although the Alexandria he describes is imaginary, Lawrence Durrell summarized the Levantine spirit in *Clea:*

. . . *the ponderous azure dream of Alexandria basking like some old reptile in the bronze Pharaonic light of the great lake. The master-sensualists of history abandoning their bodies to mirrors, to poems, to the grazing flocks of boys and women, to the needle in the vein . . . to the death-in-life of kisses without appetite. Walking those streets again in my imagination I knew once more that they spanned, not merely human history, but the whole biological scale of the heart's affections–from the painted ecstasies of Cleopatra . . . to the bigotry of Hypatia. . . . Rimbaud, student of the Abrupt Path, walked here with a belt full of gold coins. And all those other swarthy dream-interpreters and politicians and eunuchs were like a flock of birds of brilliant plumage.*

Levantine prefers to put his money into such ventures as the casino on the coast north of Beirut, below the hillside shrine of Our Lady of Lebanon, where in one lazy night oil millionaires from Kuwait or Saudi Arabia spend enough to endow 10 chairs at the university.

A world apart from such men are the Zealots of the Arab world, the men who look inward to the desert. These are the Arabs whose reaction to the West is one of opposition, even hate.

Not that zealotry is only a response to Europe. Throughout Moslem history there have been periods of what can be called fundamentalism. These periods have been reactions to laxness, mysticism and saint-worship.

A mighty fundamentalist movement started in central Arabia during the 18th Century. Its founder was the religious reformer Mohammed ibn Abdul Wahhab, who linked up with a Bedouin tribal leader, Mohammed ibn Saud. The two men agreed that if they succeeded in converting Arabia to Wahhabism, Mohammed ibn Abdul Wahhab would be the religious leader and Ibn Saud would be the sovereign. It took more than a century and many reverses before this austere, puritan movement finally succeeded. This came about in the 1920s, when Ibn Saud's descendant, Abdul Aziz ibn Saud, united most of Arabia under his rule. His kingdom embodied zealotry at its most extreme.

Under the rule of Ibn Saud, the Koran was the lawbook of Arabian society. In the time of the Prophet Mohammed no distinction had been made between "sins" and "crimes," and precise penalties had been prescribed for infractions of the divine law. This drastic letter of the Koran was followed. More liberal Moslems, objecting to such measures as public stoning for adultery, pointed out that Mohammed was an innovator in his day; nothing, therefore, could be less in accord with the Prophet's spirit than to go back to his every literal action in a different world. Such pleading fell on deaf ears in Saudi Arabia, and still does. To this day, thieves are liable to have their hands cut off, although nowadays the stump is not plunged in tar—instead, an ambulance waits with antiseptics. The decapitation of murderers is carried out in public. Women are not allowed to circulate freely in public.

Ironically, Saudi Arabia, whose barren wastes were a satisfying image to the Zealots who denounced any partnership of creature with Creator, concealed an ocean of oil. Western civilization was to descend on Saudi Arabia, but only in the form of oil drillers and oil royalties. In a later chapter this collision between money and puritanism will be considered. What is noteworthy here is how zealotry resisted—at least officially—the culture of the West. Western technology might come in, but not western customs. Princes have private movie theaters in their palaces, but the public at large is forbidden to watch motion pictures, which contravene the traditional prohibition against representing the human form.

Yemen is the stronghold of a different kind of zealotry. The Imam (the word means religious guide as much as political ruler) has one chief preoccupation, that of defending his throne against members of his own family. The climate of Yemen is more lush than that of Saudi Arabia. Feudal backwardness and suspicion of the outside world, not ideological tenets, keep the West at bay there.

The least destructive Zealots in the Arab world came, however, from a different desert. An Algerian holy man, al Senussi, studied in Mecca and then in 1837 established a religious brotherhood which later spread through the eastern half of present-day Libya. The followers of this religious movement, known as Senussis, gradually gained control of the oases—whose importance for trade was equaled by the opportunities they offered for proselytizing the desert tribes.

When the Italians invaded Libya in 1911, the Senussi sect became the backbone of resistance. In World War II thousands of Senussis fled to Egypt, where they joined the Allied forces in the struggle against Mussolini. After the war, when the Kingdom of Libya was created, Mohammed Idris al Mahdi al Senussi, the leading member of the Senussi family and a direct descendant of the founder, was made king. King Idris is a Zealot in his adherence to the old ways of Islam; in some Senussi oases women are not allowed to be seen during daylight hours.

Yet in Libya there is none of the hypocrisy visible in Saudi Arabia, and little attempt to impose Senussi ideas on others. The king lives austerely, but he does not force others to do so. He is tolerant: Jews are not allowed even to set foot in Saudi Arabia, but in Libya much of the commerce is in Jewish hands. While Christians are forbidden to visit the Saudi Arabian

THE ZEALOT'S LANDSCAPE

Charles Doughty, an English poet and archeologist, evoked the wilderness in *Travels in Arabia Deserta* (1888):

We passed the barrier cliff by a cleft banked with deep sand. The mountain backward is an horrid sandstone desolation, a death as it were and eternal stillness of nature. The mountain sandstone cloven down in cross lines, is here a maze of rhomboid masses, with deep and blind streets, as it were, of some lofty city lying between them. Of the square crags some that were softer stone are melted quite away from among them, leaving the open spaces. The heights of wasting rock are corroded into many strange forms of heads and pinnacles. The counterlines of sandstone sediment are seen at even height in all the precipices. We marched in the winter heat; a thermometer laid, upon a white cloth, upon the sand at an height of 3,700 feet, showed 86° F.

cities of Mecca and Medina, the remaining Italians in Libya are still allowed to own land. United Nations representatives, as well as members of U.S. and British overseas agencies, are able to cooperate creatively with the Libyans. It is true that a Moslem can be punished for violating the sacred month of Ramadan in public, for example by eating or smoking during daylight, but restaurants are open for Christians, and a good red wine is sold called Rosso d'Africa. In Tripoli motion-picture houses are as crowded as anywhere else in the Arab world.

The Senussis also deserve credit for their encouragement of agriculture in their oases, where they are busy tree planters. Zealots usually show marked indifference to cultivation of the soil.

All the foregoing manifestations of zealotry have an old-fashioned air to them and have little appeal for the young. There has been one modern attempt to dress zealotry up in a sophisticated form. In 1928 Hassan al Banna, an Egyptian teacher of genius, started the Moslem Brotherhood in the Egyptian city of Ismailia. Originally it had a program for social reform which made the movement popular among poverty-stricken Egyptians. But gradually it developed into a dreaded terrorist organization. At the height of its power the Brotherhood numbered more than two million; it had barracks and paramilitary formations. Al Banna's philosophy was fundamentalist; all the evils which beset the Arab world, he said, came from the Christian West. The double remedy: to go back to the first century of Islam and to exclude everything western.

THE Brotherhood became a state within the state. Politicians whom the Brotherhood disliked fell before the organization's bullets. Al Banna himself was murdered in 1949 on a Cairo sidewalk; the killers were the police, taking revenge for the murder of Prime Minister Mahmud Fahmy Nokrashy by Brotherhood members. At this time the situation in Egypt was desperate: the 1948 war with Israel had been a disaster, unemployment and poverty were on the increase, and a revolution seemed certain.

Some observers feared that the revolution, when it came, might put the Brotherhood into power.

On Black Saturday, January 26, 1952, a mob burned Cairo. In one sense the act could be interpreted as a popular upsurge, the inarticulate gesture of a downtrodden, hungry people. But the burning was extremely well organized. Young men in jeeps drove from bonfire to bonfire. No inquiry has ever clearly identified the organizers, but the carefully chosen targets—movie theaters, drinking places, the Turf Club, Shepheard's Hotel, expensive shops, cabarets—were those most odious to zealotry, and thus to the Brotherhood.

THE riots were suppressed by the army, which was to bring about Egypt's revolution six months later. At first, the Brotherhood supported the revolution. Then, suspicious that the new strongman, Gamal Abdul Nasser, was becoming too pro-western, it tried to assassinate him in Alexandria. This led to the total suppression of the Brotherhood, whose surviving limbs twitch, though without much support, as far apart as Switzerland and Jordan.

Levantines and Zealots contribute something to Arab society, but both are poisonous when they become extreme. The Levantine who capitulates to another civilization is in danger of becoming a moral exile without a soul. In a diluted form, however, he is a useful purveyor of modern ideas. Similarly, the extreme Zealot pushes Arab society toward the abyss of fanaticism. A Moslem Brotherhood victory in Egypt would have solved none of the country's basic problems. In the rage of the Brotherhood's inevitable failure, hatred of everything foreign would have been allied with religious bigotry. But a touch of zealotry can be a useful corrective, like small quantities of poison. It reminds men that there are other values than the material, and in the Arab world it reminds the Arabs that they have spiritual traditions of their own.

The scented Levantine and the uncouth Zealot are two poles: wisely most Arabs place themselves halfway between.

European and American cars surge down a street in westernized Beirut, famous for its congested business district and traffic jams.

Two Cultures in an Unlikely Harmony

The attitude of most Arabs to western ways is ambivalent. Many wish their lands to have the benefits offered by new methods in industry and farming, but few wholly admire the western-style businessmen who have made Lebanon almost a part of Europe. At the same time, although few wish to adopt the ways of the Bedouin, many admire these stiffly traditional people for helping to keep alive the Arab sense of identity and resistance to foreign cultures.

65

COSMOPOLITAN WOMEN dine with their escorts at a hotel in Cairo. The food may be eastern, but everything else—the clothing of the men and women, the easy familiarity between the sexes, the very presence of women in public—shows the impact of American and European customs on the people of the Middle Eastern cities.

DANCING COUPLES sway to American music in a hotel dining room. The clubs and roof gardens of Cairo offer entertainment including native dancers and folk music.

DEMURE MODEL parades during a fashion show *(right)*. Women have been increasingly bold in emulating western dress since a few innovators dropped the veil in 1919.

ENTREPRENEURS of the Levant provide the buildings and goods for a people now turning toward western comforts

AGGRESSIVE BUILDER from Lebanon, Emile M. Bustani *(left)* tells reporters his plan for the economic development of the Middle East. A onetime cabinet minister, Bustani runs a giant construction and trading company.

SUCCESSFUL TRADER from Arabia, Ibrahim Chakir puffs contentedly on a brass water pipe through a 15-foot, silk-covered tube in his home near Beirut. His company imports U.S. automobiles, refrigerators and plastics.

A CEREMONY OF HOSPITALITY, making coffee occurs whenever a Bedouin has a guest. The host always brews a fresh pot, the leftovers being consigned to family use.

THE IMPLEMENTS OF RITUAL, coffee-making utensils are elaborate and handsome—prized objects kept brilliantly burnished and handed down from father to son.

A GATHERING OF HERDSMEN converges on a desert water hole. Bedouin depend heavily on camels, not only for transportation, but for milk, meat and hair for weaving.

interior, the austere, nomadic Bedouin tend their herds and enjoy simple rituals

VILLAGE LIFE LINE of water is transferred from a deep canal to a local irrigation ditch by means of a cumbrous system of gears and buckets. A small boy keeps the bullock plodding around the ancient water wheel.

5

The
Immemorial
Village

ABDU'S picture has never appeared in a newspaper. He has never met a trouble shooter or a diplomat, nor has he posed for a tourist's camera, since his fields are near no important ruins. The only foreigner he has spoken to is his former grocer, an Arabic-speaking Greek. His wife's old sewing machine derives from the West, as do some U.S. advertisements with which he has plastered a wall of his house, but he has no strong feelings about the Arab attitude toward the West. He believes in God, prays five times a day in accord with the precepts of Islam, fasts during the month of Ramadan and does not expect ever to have the requisite cash

(at least $180) which would enable him to make the *hajj*, or pilgrimage, to Mecca. His uncle, who did make the *hajj*, lives next door; the walls of his whitewashed house are covered with vivid pictures of the ship and train which took him to Saudi Arabia, as well as of the people and animals he noticed on the way.

Abdu is not the camel-riding Arab of fiction, nor is he the wharfside Arab encountered in Beirut and Alexandria. He lives in a village we shall refer to as Khalidia. There is a real village named Khalidia in the undulant hills of central Egypt, near the city of Fayyum. Abdu's village resembles Khalidia and indeed is patterned after it. Khalidia illustrates some of the problems Arabs everywhere face, together with some of the changing and unchanging factors in their lives. It is in many ways typical of villages throughout the Arab world. Abdu himself is not a real person, but he is real in the sense that he typifies the Arab villager. The Arabic word used to describe him is *fellah*.

VILLAGERS, rather than Bedouin from the desert or townsmen from centers like Cairo or Damascus, constitute the overwhelming majority of Arabs. The word fellah (it is pronounced with the accent on the final syllable; its plural, fellahin, rhymes with green) has passed into western languages. This shows that the Arab fellah is in some way distinct, since otherwise "farmer" would have been used. Abdu might just as well live in the hilly coast of Morocco known as the *riff,* the Algerian *bled,* or countryside, the Egyptian delta or the great sallow trough between the Tigris and Euphrates Rivers which forms Iraq. His rhythm of life would be almost the same anywhere in the Arab world; costumes differ more than customs.

Abdu seldom thinks in national terms. His country is his village, Khalidia. It is green and lush; it is surrounded by fields which bear three crops a year; it contrasts startlingly with the pale yellow wasteland a few miles beyond the horizon. There the Bedouin roam, nomads for whom Abdu has an ancestral distrust—just as for him, the settled fellah bent over the soil, the Bedouin have an inherited contempt. In the past the Bedouin looted and killed, but with the arrival of the modern state and its police, they are hardly a cloud.

Khalidia's greenery is due to the miracle of water. Some Arab villages get their water from wells deep in the earth; those near the Mediterranean or perched in mountains get theirs from rain. Khalidia's water flows from a canal whose source is far off in a great river. The water's coming is controlled by "them"—the government and its representatives, the engineers it dispatches to the village. "They" determine how many times a month Abdu is allowed to

drench his fields to feed, in their respective seasons, his cotton, his corn, his beans.

To Abdu, "they" are aloof, wearing the different clothes and speaking in the different accent of the faraway city. Even the local town seems to him alien and not altogether safe. But to people who have come from the capital, the two or three government buildings in Khalidia, the one rickety motion-picture theater and the small hotel compose a flyblown and provincial place, unbearable for more than a night's stay on official business.

Khalidia is an interwoven world. Each house merges with the next. From afar the houses resemble cattle huddling in a storm. There is nothing individualistic about any of the houses or the people who live in them; each is a part of the whole. All are involved, as in a family, in the village of life. Just outside the village, on a brown bluff of useless land too high to irrigate, there is the village of death. Here, small brown domes and inarticulated graves mingle the village's forebears in the democracy of death. The cemetery is the abode of ghosts, a place not to be visited after dark.

Khalidia always has been Abdu's world and will be until he dies. He has visited the local town regularly throughout his life, to sell or to buy. But he has been to the capital only three times. Once was when he was summoned by the army. Another time it was to pay the rent for some additional land which he was working. The third time it was to engage a lawyer— a man from Khalidia, naturally—in a dispute over boundaries.

ABDU in middle age is tall, upright, dark from the sun, and thin. In a sense all the village is his family; but his immediate relatives are close and clearly defined. Unlike languages of the West which use the one word "cousin," Arabic has precise terms for each relationship: *ibn 'am,* son of a father's brother; *bint am,* daughter of a father's brother; *ibn khal,* son of a mother's brother; *bint khal,* daughter of a mother's brother. Similarly, there are four terms which specify the exact relationship to children of paternal and maternal aunts. These terms are important. When Abdu was a boy, he knew that he had the right to marry his paternal uncle's daughter—his *bint am*—if he should so wish. No one else could ask her hand until he had exercised his right of choice. As it happened, he did not choose to marry her; his two wives (for he divorced the first) have both been relations of his, but not first cousins. Ali, his oldest son, is almost 30. His youngest is three.

Abdu's most important relative is the headman of Khalidia. This personage lives in the largest house, made of earth like the others, but whitewashed and with plaster pillars at the door. It is called the *dawar*, or residence, a more prestigious word than *dar*, which is used for Abdu's house. The headman has a telephone and is in touch with "them." Since the expropriation of the 500 acres of an ex-prince he has been the largest landowner in the village, farming more than 50 acres. It is one of Abdu's greatest pleasures to visit this important kinsman. He sits with other villagers in the bare front room, on cotton-covered cushions on the gaunt benches, under the mottoes exalting "patience" which hang on the plastered wall. The house has running water, but since electricity is not expected until next year, the headman still makes do with impressive kerosene lamps. Abdu's own house does not have running water, though the government has recently erected a cast-iron fountain a hundred yards away down the road. Abdu's house consists of several cavernous rooms opening off a central court

ANCIENT METHODS still used on Arab farms today are shown in a painting from the 15th Century B.C. tomb of a pharaoh's field agent.

where the bread is baked; at dusk the animals, from the ducks to the water buffalo, are brought into the house for safety.

The headman is a relative whom Abdu prizes, but there are others whom he pities and helps when he can. One such is Hamouda, a brother of his first wife, who lives in a house with two windowless rooms, a cow and calf in one and his wife, three children and himself in the other. Hamouda's family sleeps on reed matting on the floor; their furniture is sparse— a large box, a small oil stove for making tea and two old lamps.

There are considerable differences of property and income in the village. Hamouda owns no land and rents two acres. Abdu himself inherited two acres from his father a number of years ago; the land of the headman is wide and shimmering. The land is the reality, and the village serves the land. The feet of all the men are incised with cracks acquired in the service of the earth. The sycamores rustle; the cotton turns white; the corn is emerald, then golden; and there is comfort for some and extreme discomfort for others. Yet all is part of a rhythm as natural as a heartbeat, and the idea that there is injustice has come only recently to the village.

Khalidia means "eternal," and the first thing that an outsider would note in Abdu's village is its eternal quality. Of course, "eternal" is a relative term. Agriculture of any kind has been known on this planet for only about 8,000 years. And Khalidia has been practicing agriculture for just about that entire time. When both New England and old England were covered with forests that had never known the hand of man, Khalidia had fellahin like Abdu and Hamouda squelching their heels in the black mud as they brought runnels of water to selected seeds and plants.

The sense of continuity with the past gives beauty. The way of life is as measured as a ballet. In the morning the village moves to the fields in a frieze of men and water buffaloes, women and sheep, boys and donkeys. While the sun climbs, the men bend over the soil with their hoes, their clothes hitched up around their waists. When the sun sinks, the animals and most of the people return. At night there are twinkling fires in the empty fields where the village guards brew tea. The crimes of the village are few and direct, having to do with women, or with crops. Feuds occur, and neighbors have been known to burn the standing corn of those they think have wronged them.

Yet there is something crushing as well as idyllic in this immemorial pattern. The pattern is so fixed that the villagers are its prisoners, not its masters. The pattern is like an old player-piano roll, long ago pierced with the right holes to play a particular tune. And today if there is need for a new music, the holes forbid it. The pattern is too strong.

YET the 20th Century has not left the village untouched. Jets from the airfields near the capital scream above the clover, hinting of problems faraway. The village's onetime absentee landlord was dispossessed as a result of an upheaval in the capital. People no longer die as young as they used to.

In the next village there is a "Combined Center," a glaringly white group of modern buildings sharply contrasting with the crumbling architectural togetherness of the village. The center has a clinic and a school, an agricultural expert and a doctor, and it has nurses and midwives who dispense drugs.

Abdu's uncle, the one who made the *hajj* to Mecca, is over 60. He often remarks to the younger men, "How the village has grown!

When I was 10, there were only a few boys to see. The rest, the boys I played with in the canal when I was younger, had all died. Now they don't die, and there are so many."

In Khalidia the pressure of the people who no longer die is palpable. The village is like a garden with the roses planted too close. Food is an obsession, for there is never enough of it. The earth is rich, but its riches must be sold. Abdu himself eats meat once or twice a month. His poor kinsman Hamouda eats meat only a few times a year, in particular at the feast which marks the end of Ramadan and the time when people celebrate the Feast of Sacrifice, which throughout the Arab world coincides with the culmination of the pilgrimage to Mecca. There have been no famines, such as those of India; Abdu is better off than many villagers elsewhere in the world. But the diet of the village is spare, and there are always new children, and new mouths.

WHEN Abdu was rejected for military service, his family rejoiced: if he had been accepted, it would have meant serving for a pittance in an army recruited for the colonial power. Now Abdu's second son has joined up, and Abdu sighs with relief. The boy will not earn much, but he will be clothed and fed. He was not bright at school; he may learn something of use as a soldier.

Abdu's only education was at the kuttab, an informal class behind the mosque in which boys were required to memorize passages from the Koran. Abdu's oldest son, Ali, went not only to school but to veterinary college. He now lives with his wife near the Combined Center. Dr. Ali presides over the veterinary section. His present preoccupation is with increasing the milk yield in the village. The village cows are *baladi*, or native: the *baladi* are recognizable in frescoes painted 3,000 years ago by Abdu's ancestors, before they were converted to Christianity and, subsequently, to Islam. The cows are gaunt, big-eyed and brown. The *baladi* cows provide five pounds of milk a day, as opposed to the 30 pounds provided by a good Friesian, a breed which flourishes in the Netherlands. A cross between a Friesian and a *baladi* does well and can yield up to 20 pounds a day. If all the fellahin could have crossbred cows, instead of the village *baladi*, the milk yield would be at least tripled. This is what "they" (including Dr. Ali) call vertical development.

But age-old Khalidia lives up to its name and the fellahin are wary of the innovations suggested by the men of the city. Hamouda has often been told that he could improve his health and that of his children with more milk. But when Dr. Ali suggests to Hamouda that his next calf should be a cross, Hamouda says flatly, "The *baladi* cow is best." Abdu's five cows are now all crosses. He accepted the idea of artificial insemination out of loyalty to his son. Other villagers are gradually accepting the idea too. In the small laboratory in the Combined Center they can see for themselves the Friesian spermatozoa like myriad glittering fish. For there is a microscope in the center, as well as a refrigerator and medicines.

Slowly, therefore, the pattern in the player-piano roll changes. But it changes too slowly to keep pace with the multiplication of children's mouths. So the minister of agriculture is to make a decree: all *baladi* bulls are to be castrated and turned into bullocks. The law will be applied, and a cross between Friesian and *baladi* will become the norm.

NOT all government fiats can be applied so easily. Ten years ago the minimum daily wage for farmhands was fixed at the equivalent of 50 cents a day, and slightly higher for other workers. It has recently been increased to 75 cents for industrial workers. But because the population is so large, there are idle hands who willingly accept far less. A landowner has no difficulty in finding fellahin who will accept 25 cents. When Abdu needs extra hands to gather his crops at harvest time, he cannot afford to offer more.

But change is eroding the immemorial pattern. A new intermezzo in the village rhythm is the noon exodus of children, hundreds and hundreds of them, from school. Primary education is now almost universal, in fact and theory. The children may be earth-stained, their books may be worn, but their minds are acquiring the potentially explosive force of education.

PEASANT revolts have not been a feature of Arab villages. But the next generation will be literate. This fact may destroy the age-old image of the docile fellah. The city student has always been a potential political agitator—an agitator often destructive, but at the same time vital. Teachers now come to the village. They replace the bigoted village preacher and the wisewoman as sources of information. In the future, injustice will no longer be passively endured as it has been in the past. It will be revolted against. The fellahin do not wish to be picturesque.

Change fills the schools, castrates the *baladi* bulls and brings bigger crop yields, thanks to better seeds and the use of fertilizers, as well as bigger eggs, thanks to the Rhode Island Reds imported from the U.S. Change has brought a radio to the Khalidia coffee shop where, by flaring lamp in the evening, Abdu plays *konkan* (a kind of rummy) with his friends. But change only emphasizes the Malthusian thesis that population increases at a faster rate than agricultural production. There is a bigger village cake, but at the same time there are more mouths open for crumbs.

No easy answers exist for such problems. "Mechanization of agriculture" is a slogan popular with the young. But tractors would merely put more fellahin out of work; in most Arab countries there is no lack of manpower.

"Birth control on a national scale" is a remedy popular with foreign visitors. Islam does not condemn the practice of birth control as sternly as does the Roman Catholic Church, but it does not endorse it. The real obstacle lies in popular attitudes. An Egyptian Jesuit of Lebanese origin, Father Henry Ayrout, wrote many years ago, when Abdu was a boy, "The men understand only sexual love. They revel in it, each with his own wife, and are kept faithful less by virtue than by village law. Adultery leads immediately to bloodshed, and prostitutes are beyond their means. The heat of passion is short-lived. At 30 a fellah woman is no longer attractive, but the children she has borne her husband bind him to her. Both want children above everything else. To the wife they mean social prestige, for barrenness is a disgrace and the chief cause of polygamy and divorce. To the father they represent helpers and successors, who will allow him to rest and give orders. Accordingly families are large." These words are still largely true of all Arab villagers. To remove the fellah's desire for children is not simple today. Nor will it be tomorrow.

THE only solution to rural overpopulation lies in emigration to the cities. To the people of Khalidia, the city glitters mirage-bright beyond the railway, to the north. There even the poor seem rich.

Two of Abdu's brothers migrated to the capital. They, too, form part of a rhythm: shanty towns of mud or tin encircle most Arab capitals, for the housing shortage is even greater than the food shortage. In the city the villagers begin to adapt themselves to modern ways, exchanging the *gallabeya* (the loose cotton robe called *dishdasha* in Iraq) for trousers and shirt; more slowly they discard their rural attitudes. When they sit in a café, it is one where they can meet friends from home. Each village has a café of its own.

The brothers were not particularly pleased to leave. Today they eagerly ask each arrival from Khalidia for news, and they have taken to the capital the attitudes of the village—the industriousness, the willingness to work together, the patience which is the *baladi* virtue. So long as the city can offer them jobs, they can offer the city a valuable element and can create industrial wealth to offset rural dearth. But if the city fails to create jobs for them, they and thousands like them can in one season turn into members of a seething proletariat, themselves desperate and ready to support desperate men.

Abdu is too old and too fixed in his ways to migrate to the city; besides, he loves his land. His attitude to his two acres is exactly the same as that of the chief character in *Egyptian Earth,* an English translation of a novel published in Egypt in 1954. This fellah possesses only one acre: "The earth itself seemed to him a symbol of strength, of that which will endure forever, and of honor. . . . He knew it all, he knew every inch of it, every detail. This land was his own life and his own history. When a boy [he] had been given a little hoe, the same tool that his father had carried before him. And when he had grown up, and his father had died, the hoe had grown too. He knew the history of this land, of its crops, of its beasts, since the time he had first tethered a buffalo . . . that had been when he was eight . . . he remembered hammering the wedge into the earth. Not one detail connected with this land would he ever forget, and after him his son would inherit his memories with the land itself. . . . The land never let you down. His father had planted berseem [clover], had changed to cotton, then to beans, or perhaps sugar cane, and always the land was generous, if you were generous to the land. If you were faithful to the land, if you tended it and cared for it, it would care for you. An acre . . . a separate acre: it gave him a special standing in the village."

ABDU has such standing in Khalidia with his two acres. But when he dies, his land will be automatically divided among his sons and daughters according to the inheritance laws of the Koran: two shares to a male, one share to a female. His children will not have enough to give them a special standing in the village, let alone a livelihood.

So Khalidia goes on in its eternal ways. But this will not be for long. Within a generation there will be an explosion of the immemorial. The only question: will it be a creative one, like the explosion in a gasoline engine, or will it be anarchy, the bursting of a pressure cooker? The children clutching the textbooks in their hands will answer that.

The close-packed houses of a small farm village in Upper Egypt gain shelter from the burning sun in a grove of slender palm trees.

A Grim Struggle for a Meager Living

Arab farmers wring sustenance from the soil against terrible odds. In most Arab lands the sun burns down with searing heat. Rainfall is generally inadequate, and vast tracts of desert will be forever barren. Irrigation has made only a fraction of the land arable, and this fraction is increasingly overpopulated and overworked. Many farmers have tiny plots unsuitable for modern farm methods. Yet Arab farmers love the land and work it carefully and lovingly.

A FRUGAL MEAL of maize bread, a staple of peasant life, is eaten by an Egyptian farming family. The straw mat on which they sit also serves as a bed for the parents.

A MIDDAY REST is enjoyed by three Arab women (*opposite*) and a goat on an arbor-shaded porch. Fellahin women often wear black robes over their other clothing.

GRUBBING A HARVEST by hand, farmers squat on their heels in a field near the Nile. The most important crops on Egyptian farms are cotton, clover and food grains.

GUARDING A FLOCK, a shepherd prods his precious sheep from an outlying pasture to the safety of the village at sunset. Scarce pasturage limits the size of flocks.

PUMPING WATER, an Arab farmer works a device reputedly invented by Archimedes in the Third Century B.C. The tube contains a rotating screw which sucks up water.

STEEL ARTERIES carrying oil through the vast Sahara emerge aboveground near an Algerian oil center where excess gas is being flared away in flame-plumed towers. Nearly half of all the world's known oil lies in Arab lands.

6

Fuel
for an
Arid Economy

OIL, the most valued fuel of the 20th Century, is the greatest single prize of the Arab world. Geologists estimate that nearly half of the earth's known reserves are contained in the Arab nations. There, where it has been exploited for scarcely two decades, oil has suddenly and dramatically juxtaposed extreme wealth with the desert landscape that had been for centuries the very symbol of dearth. Above all, the discovery of oil, and the new source of capital it represented, provided the opportunity of bringing 20th Century irrigation methods to long-barren land. Oil and water are now the warp and woof of which the Arab economy and Arab society are increasingly being woven.

Less than 6 per cent of the Arab lands can currently be cultivated; in some countries, such as Libya, optimistic estimates are that, with presently known water reserves, only around 1 per cent of the soil can eventually be put under the plow. Even this estimate, however, is based on the assumption that the plow will be a light one, since the friable sandy earth blows away in the form of sandstorms when standard plows are used.

Before the discovery of the first Arab oil, there seemed little for man to do with the desert but accept it. Of course, with capital and skill it was possible to make anything grow in the light soil under the bountiful sun —if water was available. But capital was always scarce, and agriculture developed only in the oases. With the majority of deserts, there was nothing for the Arabs to do but use them— like the seas—as highways for traveling or game reserves for hunting.

The landscape of Arabia and Syria, of Libya and the great Sahara itself imposed its own conditions. The Bedouin way of life was not adopted for its picturesque quality nor from any innate love of freedom. It developed as the only way in which man could stay alive in the desert's lunar inhospitality; he depended on his animals, and these had to move from vegetation to scanty vegetation.

The desert not only imposed a nomadic way of life; it also imposed certain values and certain virtues.

THE desert was of its nature capricious. Sudden showers would occur; torrents would flow through the eroded wadis; and in the plains the Arabs would plant crops and rejoice if they came to fruition. They learned not to be surprised if the barley withered almost as soon as it appeared. The very shapes of the dunes constantly changed. Wells which were sweet one year might by the next season become brackish, or they might fill with sand. The desert taught its sons to trust in fate, but to accept fate's death sentences when they were issued. There was none of the land husbandry which distinguishes the western farmer or the Egyptian fellah. You became rich: it was the blessing of God. You were abruptly poor: it was God's new test. The idea of keeping accounts, of balancing budgets, was as alien to the desert as refrigeration.

The desert was dangerous. Other men might save your life if you were dying of thirst; you would save theirs in a similar crisis. Hence the hospitality of the nomads and its extension to fantastic limits. The enemy who had killed your brother was to be given food and shelter for three days and no questions asked.

Over the centuries, the Bedouin wandered their own way, hardly affected by the Turks or later by the European imperialists who took over from them. The Ottomans sent occasional armies into Arabia, but they never exercised genuine control. There was no advantage to be gained in doing so. The same was true in North Africa, where the nomadic Tuareg continued to deal in slaves and to tax the trans-Saharan caravans long after French rule had been officially established to the north and south.

THE Arab country which first witnessed the avalanche of coin produced by petroleum was the puritanical kingdom of Saudi Arabia. When Abdul Aziz ibn Saud united his jigsaw collection of deserts between 1906 and 1930, the captured cities of Mecca and Medina represented his major source of income, since the rulers of the Moslem Holy Land had long fleeced the pious. During its first decade Ibn Saud's impoverished realm was a model of puritan rigor. The penalties for theft were extreme. It was said that you could leave a purse in the streets of Riyadh and find it intact in the same place the following day.

Then in 1938 oil was found in substantial quantities near Dhahran, agreements with an American oil company were implemented, and after World War II the transformation began— not of Arabia itself, but of the king and his royal family. Royalties—the king obtained 50 per cent of all profits, with no action on his part—went direct to the kingly coffers; there was no system of accounting. Once simple men who had seized power with old-fashioned carbines, men who had known what it was to hunger, the Saudi Arabian sheiks became oriental potentates with the magic key to the West's treasure chest.

In Beirut, in Europe and in America, Saudi princes became famous or notorious in hotels, cabarets, shops—wherever money was conspicuously spent. Palaces, luxurious cars and imported women became the status symbols of what was by then a royal tribe, for Ibn Saud had married more than a hundred women, and his sons had imitated their father. The royal family of the second and third generations was numbered in the thousands.

Ibn Saud was a physical giant. There was nothing malicious or calculated in his waste of what would be regarded in more-developed countries as public funds. A simple man, he was totally unequipped by his upbringing and his experience to cope with the deluge of money.

The old warrior was succeeded by his son, Saud, a man far less impressive than his father. Under him, the oil royalties were spent in yet more openly wasteful fashion. Abroad, Saudi money was disbursed on bribes, on subventions to assassins and in such dissipation that in Cairo Saudi became a synonym for debauchery. At home, palaces comparable to Versailles were erected in the desert capital of Riyadh. Instead of spending the oil revenues to utilize the frail water resources of the arid Arabian peninsula to develop agriculture while the capital was available, the Saudi potentates imported modern pumps which rapidly sucked up the underground water, itself possibly as old as oil. The water table around Riyadh, once high enough for peasant wells worked by donkeys, sank lower and lower while splashing, floodlit fountains in the royal gardens amused the princes and their friends. There was a danger not only that morals were being corrupted by the abundant cash, and the oil reserves wasted for nothing, but that water itself was being spent in such a way that it could never be replenished.

An irony of the Saudi prodigality—and one hardly noticed by other Arab countries which denounced it—was that the managers of the United States-owned Arabian American Oil Company were doing precisely what the Arab nationalists had always insisted on: keeping strictly out of Arab affairs. Aramco did not interfere at all with the king's business. Its directors believed they were there to make money out of the oil and to pay for it, honorably. They did both. They paid the king promptly and, while they gave technical assistance when asked, they did nothing that might suggest that they were trying to influence him.

Things have been handled differently higher up the Persian Gulf. The tiny 6,000-square-mile state of Kuwait, once famous only for pearl divers, lies over an oil lake vaster than any in Saudi Arabia. There a perceptive ruler, Sheik Abdullah al Sabah, in alliance with the United States- and British-owned Kuwait Oil Company, has done much for the people. The free schools, hospitals and dental clinics are as good as any in the world. The major criticism that might be made is that the remainder of the vast sums given Sheik Abdullah was mainly invested in London rather than in the development of other Arab nations. Thus Kuwait was like a glittering patch of new cloth in a seedy garment. The ultimate paradox: the city of Kuwait itself, where everyone could aspire to driving a car but where there was nowhere to drive except back and forth within the state.

Emile Bustani, the Lebanese entrepreneur, was the first to suggest that places like Kuwait (whose annual income of $500 million was far in excess of the needs of its 321,000 people) should invest at least part of their revenues in other Arab countries. A remarkable fact about Kuwait is that this suggestion did not fall on closed ears. In 1961 Kuwait established a government fund to make loans for development projects in other Arab countries. As many Arabs have pointed out, it is absurd for countries like Egypt to have to borrow from either

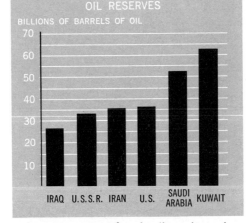

OIL RESERVES
BILLIONS OF BARRELS OF OIL

IRAQ U.S.S.R. IRAN U.S. SAUDI ARABIA KUWAIT

BIGGEST SOURCES of crude oil are shown in a graph of proved reserves—the amount experts believe is potentially available for extraction.

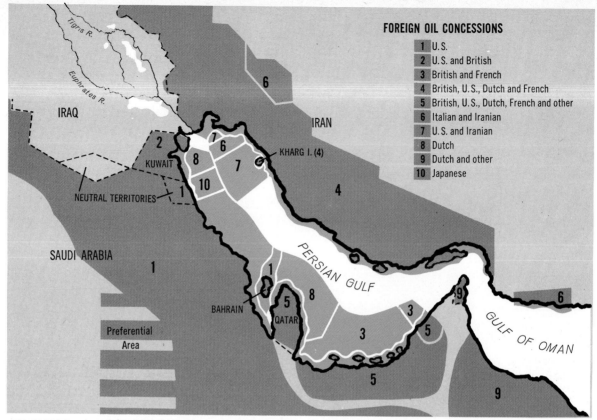

FOREIGN OIL CONCESSIONS

1 U.S.
2 U.S. and British
3 British and French
4 British, U.S., Dutch and French
5 British, U.S., Dutch, French and other
6 Italian and Iranian
7 U.S. and Iranian
8 Dutch
9 Dutch and other
10 Japanese

OIL RIGHTS granted by Middle Eastern powers in the Persian Gulf area to foreign producing and marketing organizations are shown here. Concessions are in green; numbers indicate the foreign country or countries concerned. U.S. interests are maintained by private firms, but some others are held partially or entirely by governments.

West or East when money exists in vast quantities inside the Arab world itself.

Only one relatively advanced Arab country has so far undergone the experience of receiving large oil revenues. Iraq had been the first of the countries to find major oil deposits. Revenues began to come in on a modest scale in 1935, but it was only after World War II that they became considerable. Between 1949 and 1960 they rose from nine million dollars a year to $266 million. Pipelines were built across the Syrian desert to the Mediterranean, to obviate sending the oil to Europe and the United States via the Persian Gulf and then around the Arabian peninsula through the Suez Canal.

Iraq, in constant revolt under the British mandate, had become an independent state and a member of the League of Nations by 1932. Feisal, one of the sons of Hussein, the Hashemite ruler of Mecca, was made king and a constitution drawn up. But the parliament became a facade, representing the landowners who supported the British connection. They stifled any attempt at radical reforms. At the same time, there was a free press, and education had expanded rapidly. Constant demonstrations and riots troubled Baghdad and Basra. Public opinion could not impose a democratic government, but it did prevent the Hashemite monarchy from playing with the oil money in the manner of the unhampered Saudis. Nuri Said, the elderly and pro-British prime minister, was not without skill or vision. In 1950 he set up a Development Board to invest capital acquired from oil in large-scale projects. Iraq's share of oil profits had increased to 50 per cent in 1952 as a direct result of the nationalization of the Anglo-Iranian Oil Company by the prime minister of neighboring Iran, Mohammed Mossadegh. There were prospects that Iraqi royalties would reach $200 million a year by 1956. This was an immense sum in a country of five million people which had a total national income of only $600 million a year.

The Development Board, accepted by the parliament of landowners, was a major achievement of Nuri Said. It was not a total success. Nuri had no understanding of the need for popular consultation. The benefits provided by the board were potentially immense but all long-term. Small projects, which could have brought immediate benefit to the ordinary farmer and townsman, were rejected for mammoth schemes remote from the cities.

THE board's schemes were nonetheless important. They showed for the first time a governmental awareness that, rightly used, oil could buy—through the construction of dams, canals and pumps—the water which is the real need of the Middle East.

From remotest history, the treacherous, swift-rising river Tigris had been as savage as its name. Unlike the kindly Nile, which floods in late summer just when the farmers need extra water, the Tigris floods in spring, soon after the snow melts in the highlands of Iran and Turkey, where the river has its source. Sometimes the floods were so great that Baghdad, Iraq's capital on the Tigris, was itself threatened with inundation. And because floods were impossible to predict, it was also impossible to make efficient use of the water. If the natural basins and marshlands in the areas southeast of Baghdad were full, the new flood waters simply ran unchecked over the land; if there was no flood, then there were empty basins and no water for the furnace summer.

By 1956 the Development Board had largely solved the problem. The Tigris' flood waters were diverted into a channel which led to a vast natural depression, there to evaporate in peace. But Baghdad, freed from flood danger, was not freed from distrust.

Nuri had bound himself to the 1955 British-sponsored Baghdad Pact, which linked Iraq to Turkey, Iran and Pakistan for mutual defense against the Soviet Union. This "Northern Tier" pact was opposed by Egypt and by the majority of Arabs. When in 1956 Britain and France attacked Egypt after President Gamal Abdul Nasser's nationalization of the Suez Canal, Nuri's fate was sealed. In July 1958, the three chief figures of the old Iraq—young King Feisal II, his crafty uncle, Prince Abdul Ilah, and Nuri—were all in Baghdad at once. On the morning of July 14, just before all three men left for Istanbul to attend a Baghdad Pact meeting, the soldiers of Abdul Karim Kassem, commander of an Iraqi army brigade, surrounded the palace where the king and his uncle had slept and shot them as they stepped out the door. Nuri himself, badly disguised in the black robe of a Moslem woman, attempted escape; he was recognized and killed. With his death, the board's schemes went into neutral gear.

The Arab country in which oil and water have confronted each other most recently is Libya. In so arid a country all agriculture is bound to be difficult, although the rewards for success can be great, as the Italians proved before World War II (for their benefit, of course, not that of the Libyans). They turned semi-desert areas into astonishingly beautiful replicas of Italy's countryside, with windbreaks of cypresses arresting erosion. This required a loving toil by farmers who regarded the soil with the same tenderness which a man feels for his wife—in a word, husbandry.

THE Italian tradition of husbandry never took root in Libya. The modern Libyans have no agricultural traditions. They are still a pastoral people, preferring to graze goats and sheep rather than to work the land. Most observers agree that when Libyans buy farms previously owned by Italians, there is a sharp drop in efficiency.

The granting of independence to Libya was one of the earliest achievements of the United Nations after World War II. With genuine idealism many Westerners worked in this vast territory, which contains only a little more than a million people. The country had few resources and a lack of trained personnel. Yet some experts believed that the Libyans might achieve a decent sufficiency by re-establishing agriculture in the limited areas where it was possible. "There is general agreement," an American expert wrote, "that Libya's ultimate source of economic strength, second only to the capabilities of the people themselves, lies in agriculture—the development, conservation and utilization of the resources in land and water. Regardless of whether or not total national income from other sources might for a limited time exceed that derived from agricultural pursuits, certain it is that, for the foreseeable future, more people will derive their livelihood from agriculture and activities stemming directly from it than from all other fields of economic activity combined."

A DEVOTION to agriculture can be aroused in Arabs as much as in other people. In Egypt the desert is being devoured in massive annual bites; fields rich in tomatoes and lettuce grow where sand drifted only five years ago. There is a chain of oases in the Western Desert. In them optimistic young Egyptians hope to tap a subterranean Nile to reclaim a "new valley," comparable in importance to the old.

But in Libya the problem has been magnified greatly by the discovery of oil in 1959. Concessions have been granted to numerous oil companies. Libya has become potentially rich.

The Libyan challenge presents itself in concrete terms to individuals. A man named Saad, now in his early thirties, was one of the few Libyans who achieved a rudimentary education under the Italians. After the war, a scholarship took him to an agricultural college in Texas. He liked America, danced with American girls and learned customs which not only pleased him but had in his eyes the enhanced value of status symbols. He returned to Libya with his diploma in 1956. His salary as an agricultural expert advising new farmers was large by Libyan standards; but it could not buy him an American way of living. Furthermore, his job required him to live, not in convenient Tripoli, but in a village 40 miles out. There was no motion-picture theater; the evenings were dull.

But when the oil was discovered, Saad found a different life. The newly arrived oil companies needed educated Libyans. Their knowledge of Arabic and local customs was useful, and it was policy to employ local labor. Saad's diploma already set him apart; when he accepted an oil company's offer to work as a public relations officer, he entered a yet more precious elite, one which was highly paid. Today he has a six-room house, a wife learning English (though she still does not appear in public) and a small garden in which he never works. The post of agricultural adviser which he had held in the village is still unfilled.

Saad already has two daughters and a son; it is possible that when they grow up they will be citizens of a country with hardly any agriculture at all—a country primed on oil but failing to produce even the simplest foodstuffs, which will have to be bought from Italy or neighboring Tunisia. The Libyans who do not have university degrees will exist in a state of poverty tidied up by doles.

OIL can fuel a magic lamp. Everything depends on what boon the craver asks. It has brought the Arab world capital, not only for the mammoth schemes which so impress national governments, but for a hundred modest but vital things, ranging from concrete to line the irrigation ditches (much of the water may be lost if there is no lining), to sprinklers that diffuse the water with the greatest effectiveness. On the other hand, oil has removed the incentive to struggle; it has bought the fastest ticket to demoralization, to luxury without work.

Egypt, the most advanced Arab state, does not have enough oil for its own needs. Its achievements may well have been furthered by the need to make economies at every step and to consider any scheme, however small, that might promote production. Whether oil is an ultimate blessing or a curse in the Arab world is yet to be decided. But wherever there is water, there is the possibility of life. If oil can serve water, it can help conquer the desert, which held life a prisoner so long.

Traversing a welcome mat of rich Persian rugs, Saudi Arabia's King Saud arrives in a Cadillac on the terrace of a royal palace.

A Burst of Wealth in Arid Wastelands

One of the unhappy paradoxes of Arabian oil is that it lies thickest where it benefits the fewest people. In Egypt there is barely enough of it; in desert fiefdoms it gushes out like pipe dreams of glory. It has given tiny Kuwait more wealth than it can handle; in Saudi Arabia it has engulfed princes in a sea of extravagance. Only when oil riches are used to produce new farms and factories will the unexpected windfall become a general boon to the Arab world.

A RICH ENCLAVE in the desert,

Kuwait is ruled by a sheik

who has turned his once-destitute land

into a prosperous welfare state

SHEIKLY HOSPITALITY is offered at the palace by Kuwait's ruler, a traditional patriarch with a billion-dollar treasury at his disposal.

BOOM-TOWN NEON spangles the port of Kuwait *(opposite)*, whose inhabitants now enjoy one of the world's highest per capita incomes.

COPIOUS OVERFLOW of food from the sheik's luncheon *(below)* provides a hearty meal for the household's butlers, servants and drivers.

A CEASELESS OUTPOURING of oil is creating

a vast reservoir of sorely needed capital that

may some day help wipe out the poverty of the desert

ON GUARD at an exposed point along an oil pipeline, armed Bedouin keep watch against marauders. Pipelines constitute inviting targets for antiforeign extremists.

ON THE MOVE across a desert that holds more oil than water, a few of Arabia's dwindling number of nomadic herders keep up their endless search for fresh pasturage.

MOLTEN IRON glows hotly as it pours out of a Cairo blast furnace into a deep trough. Well supplied with iron ore, Egypt is now investing heavily in primary industries to cut down its dependence on foreign steel imports.

7

Egypt: The Potent Center

UNIFORMED motorcyclists announce his coming. "Champion of Arabism!" chant half a million throats, "Hero of Socialism!" An open car slowly passes through the choked streets of Cairo, sirens screaming. Adept gentlemen, automatics invisible in their drape suits, slouch on the bumpers. Inside, standing beside Nehru of India, Tito of Yugoslavia or Sukarno of Indonesia, smiles a hefty Egyptian, as dark as Tutenkhamen, but with the build of an athlete. The car is forced to a halt as the crowds overwhelm it, the variegated crowds of the Middle East, capable of enthusiasm, capable of burning down a city: crowds which for

10 years have not organized strikes or antigovernment demonstrations. Gamal Abdul Nasser waves and the car proceeds—past the Bab al Hadeed railroad station where stands the massive statue of Ramses II, through the 19th Century heart of modern Cairo, and finally to Liberation Square, where the Nile Hilton occupies the site of a former British barracks.

Nearly a century ago, the early Pan-Islamist leader, Jamal al Din al Afghani, wrote, "The faithful look upon Egypt as part of the holy lands. It has a place in their hearts which no other country can occupy." To the modern Arab, the religious phraseology might sound quaint—but he would echo the sentiment. Cairo has become the heart of Arabism, and the Nile Valley the focus of all Arab movements. And in recent years the personality of Gamal Abdul Nasser has made such a strong imprint both on Egypt and on its neighbors that any examination of the Arab world today must take into account the man himself and the political movement he has led.

IT is primarily because of what he symbolizes that Egyptians take such delight in seeing Nasser and listening to him. For if their president has made more impact inside the Arab world than any figure since Saladin, the warrior who defeated the Crusaders in the 12th Century, he is also the first Arab of modern times to become a world figure. Egyptians hear frequently from their president. He speaks whenever there is a crisis, or on the anniversary of the 1952 revolution which brought him to power. City squares are turned gaudy with bunting, jammed with thousands of chairs. Nasser speaks in his haunting, unpedantic, local Arabic dialect—deliberately sidestepping the custom of speaking publicly in classical Arabic. From Aswan to Alexandria he comes alive on television screens in middle-class parlors and working-class cafés. The speeches may last for hours, drinks are sold in the squares, women kick off their tight shoes, the people listen. Will it be a recitation of past struggles? Or will some new announcement affect their livelihood and their pride? There is a pleasurable sense of "perhaps."

In 1954 Abdul Nasser just missed assassination in an Alexandria square. In 1956, from the same square, he announced the nationalization of the Suez Canal, dug by the ancestors of his listeners. In 1961 he decreed a whole series of socialist measures designed to effect a second stage in the revolution. A few months later, when these measures became major factors in the secession of Syria from the United Arab Republic, which the two nations had established less than four years earlier *(Chapter 8)*, Abdul Nasser spoke with tears in his voice and

a restraint rare in rebuffed statesmen: he would not use force to reimpose an Arab union which had been voted by free consent. It is not surprising that the expectant crowds wonder what he will say next.

To a people long used to leaders taking their orders from foreign embassies, it is a pleasure in itself to have a leader on whose word foreign embassies now hang. Abdul Nasser may be hated, feted and flattered, but above all he is taken seriously. Arabs recall that Anthony Eden tried to knock him off his perch when Britain and France invaded Egypt duing the 1956 Suez Canal crisis; it was the British prime minister who fell, not the Egyptian president. That was in itself a revolution.

The glamor of their young leader, handsomer in their eyes than other statesmen, has rubbed off on the Egyptians—who have always liked a radiant center. They even loved King Farouk before he became the fat, sybaritic monarch whom Nasser and his men deposed in 1952. And the crowds used to chant "Nahas Pasha!" in honor of the once-great nationalist leader of the 1930s as enthusiastically as they now chant "Nasser!" But it is Nasser, not Farouk or Nahas Pasha, who gave them a passport of which—if they get an exit visa—they can be proud.

TO the Arabs, Nasser exists on three levels. First of all, he is a typical Egyptian family man, eating *ful mudammas* (boiled and seasoned fava beans) for breakfast, listening to the Cairo Radio singer Um Kalthum on Thursday evenings, fasting during Ramadan, praying on Fridays, collecting jokes against himself. He has the Egyptian sense of humor which is unique in the Arab world; to Egyptians, most of the other Arabs have *dam ta'eel* (heavy blood). He has a wife, three daughters and two sons.

On a second level, Nasser is non-Egyptian, a man possessed of a dedication and determination rare in a people whose usual character is capricious as well as humorous. He showed powers of secrecy beyond the capacity of most

Arabs when he planned the conspiracy against Farouk over a period of 10 years and managed to keep it secret in the gossipy Middle East—so secret that 300 officers (including an inner ring of nine) never disclosed their plans. This conspiracy did much for Egypt, but it may have harmed Nasser himself, since it has left him suspicious of nearly everyone.

ON a third level, there is Nasser the legend: the dragon slayer, the Saladin of today. Public photographs usually depict the legend, showing either a dreamy officer in a large military hat (the first popular portrait) or a movie star with a toothpaste smile. The legend makes it hard to uncover facts, even such simple ones as where he was born. Some authorities claim that Beni Murr was his birthplace; his father, a postmaster in Alexandria, was certainly born there. Beni Murr is a farming village in Upper, or southern, Egypt, and some of those who foster the legend wish to make Nasser the son of a fellah. Other authorities (including so official a source as a pamphlet published by the government Information Department in Cairo) say that he was born on Doctor-Anawati Street, in the Alexandrian suburb of Bacos.

Such quibbles are unimportant. There are undisputed facts about Gamal Abdul Nasser that are more meaningful. In his family background he is lower middle-class. His father, son of an Upper Egyptian fellah family, managed to acquire some education and so climb the first rungs of middle-class life. From his father, Abdul Nasser Hussein, Nasser inherited the Upper Egyptian temperament—fiery, loyal, jealous, tougher than that of the people of the Nile Delta and more quick-tempered. From his mother, whom he lost as a boy and dearly loved, he perhaps inherited the power of mastering his emotions, a quality also rare among Egyptians. Nasser's main feature for those who caricature him is his emphatic nose. It is an Arab rather than an Egyptian nose, for he comes of Arab stock. The name of his ancestral village, Beni Murr, originally settled by Arabs, means "the Tribe of the Bitter."

The critical dates in Nasser's life coincided with important political events. He was born in 1918, the year World War I ended. This was the signal for a period of struggle in Egypt against the British, who had controlled it since the occupation of 1882 (Chapter 3). A delegation (in Arabic wafd) of Egyptian politicians asked to go to the Paris Peace Conference after the war to demand the independence of their country; they were led by the founder of the Wafd party, Saad Zaghloul. The British reply was to exile the Wafdist leaders. The Egyptians retaliated with nationwide strikes and violence. Ultimately, in 1922, the British declared a formal end to their protectorate and granted Egypt nominal independence.

As Nasser grew into young manhood, the reputations of Egyptian politicians declined, with good reason. After Zaghloul's death in 1927, the Wafd passed into the hands of Mustafa Nahas, often called Nahas Pasha. At first a respected nationalist leader, Nahas later became the tool of the British. In February 1942, in order to form a stable government to their liking, the British drove tanks through the gates of Abdin palace, the royal residence in Cairo, and forced Farouk to accept Nahas as his prime minister. By so doing, they ruined both Egypt's monarchy (which from then on was despised because the king had lost face) and Egypt's parliamentary system (which from then on was distrusted). During these years the rich became conspicuously richer and the poor more desperately poor.

THE young Nasser was obsessed with politics, like all Egyptians at that time—but more so. He was solemn, studious. His heroes were the Prophet Mohammed; Mustafa Kamil, a pre-World War I Egyptian nationalist; and Mohandas Gandhi, whom he admired more for his struggle against the rule of the British in India than for Gandhi's philosophy of nonviolence. In his youth, he toyed with the Egyptian variants of philosophies then tempting mankind: Communism, which he rejected for its atheism; Fascism, in the form of the Misr al

Fatat, or Young Egypt, party, whose ideas were modeled on those of Mussolini's Fascists; and religious fundamentalism in the form of the fanatical Moslem Brotherhood.

For his career, young Nasser first applied for admission to the Egyptian Royal Military Academy, Egypt's West Point; but when his application was rejected, he chose law, a road popular with his generation and his class. He attended the law school of Fuad University (now called Cairo University), but he read few law books. He left the school and on a second try was granted admission to the military academy.

There is some irony in Nasser's entry into the military academy. It had been redesigned in 1882 to protect the throne after the revolt led by Arabi Pasha, in which the academy cadets had participated. Only boys from "suitable" homes were accepted—those who would identify their interests with those of the king and the ruling class. But the Wafd government, with the approval of the British (later to be Nasser's opponents), now took steps to admit cadets from other social classes. It was 1936, the year after Mussolini's occupation of Ethiopia.

The young men who attended the military academy with Nasser are ruling Egypt with him today. From the beginning, Nasser began creating a nexus of cells whose members were known only to himself, with the general objective of making a change. Though he was a revolutionary, he would not go further than this with the members of his movement. He discouraged discussion of ideology. An element of pragmatism was a feature of his character. He once said that he reacted rather than acted.

WORLD WAR II was a period of depression for the young officers. They felt themselves uninvolved; they were bitter when Winston Churchill ordered the Egyptian army to be withdrawn from Mersa Matruh, a strategic point in the Western Desert, after the Italian armies had rolled into Egypt.

Minor and major humiliations from British "advisers" faded to insignificance in the fiasco of the Palestine war. The Egyptian army was sent to Palestine to fight the new state of Israel in May 1948 as if to a picnic; its arms were defective, its supply hopeless, its strategy nonexistent. Nasser and his fellow officers believed that what interested their government was not the fate of the Palestine Arabs, but the cheap prestige of a quick victory over Israel. Besieged in the town of Falluja some 35 miles from Tel Aviv, Nasser concluded that the enemy lay at home: "Over there is our country, a far, far bigger Falluja," he later wrote. "What was happening in Falluja was only what was happening in Egypt. . . . She too had been besieged by difficulties, as well as ravaged by an enemy. She too had been cheated and pushed into a fight for which she was not prepared. Greed, intrigue and passion had used her as a plaything, too, and had placed her under fire, without arms."

ANYONE who knew Egypt between 1948 and 1952 knew it as a land of despair; no one, not even the king himself, believed that the monarchy could last. The only question: who would inherit the mess? The Moslem Brotherhood, with its fanatical zealotry? The Communists, with their made-in-Moscow planning? Few considered the army, which had long been identified with the monarchy.

The burning of Cairo by disaffected elements on January 26, 1952 *(Chapter 4)*, alerted the world to the imminence of a revolution; it alerted the Free Officers, as Nasser had named his groups, to the need to act.

Action was taken on July 23, 1952, when the king was in Alexandria; Cairo was captured by the Free Officers under the ostensible command of General Mohammed Naguib (Nasser was the real leader). Only two men were killed.

Over the next nine years a political revolution was accomplished in phases. First, the king was exiled in favor of his baby son, Ahmed Fuad II. Next year he, too, was dethroned and Egypt declared a republic.

Second, the British hold on Egypt was broken after 72 years. An agreement was signed in 1954, and by 1956 the last British troops had left. At the same time, Farouk's pretensions to being

King of the Sudan were abandoned, and Egypt and Britain jointly conceded the Sudanese their independence.

Third, the power of the landowning oligarchy was broken; a land-reform law was passed two months after the revolution. This was not Socialist; it confirmed the principle of private ownership, but restricted land holdings to a maximum of 200 acres. (In 1961, holdings were restricted to 100 acres.)

Fourth, Nasser used his near-assassination in Alexandria in 1954 to break, once and for all, the power of the Moslem Brotherhood. This was the only time that he personally endorsed political executions; six leaders of the Brotherhood were hanged for participating in the plot against his life. Naguib, who was accused of implication in the plot, was arrested and Nasser assumed overt control of the government.

Fifth, Egypt signed an arms agreement with Czechoslovakia and the Soviet Union. This was made after the failure of negotiations with the United States which, after trying to enroll Egypt in a western defense bloc, insisted that United States arms made available to Egypt be accompanied by an American military advisory group. The purpose of this provision was to make certain that the arms could not be used aggressively. This Nasser considered an infringement on Egyptian sovereignty.

Sixth, the Suez Canal Company was nationalized in 1956 and kept nationalized in the face of Anglo-French intervention. Nationalization was in response to the withdrawal by the United States and Britain of an offer to help build the Aswan High Dam; but Nasser had long envisaged the step, which accounts for the smoothness of the takeover. The canal was run more smoothly than before, and also more profitably.

ALL these were political victories; they were the fulfillment of the dreams of articulate Egyptians; at the same time their fruits (with the exception of the Suez Canal revenues) were unusable. The problems of Egypt were not political only: they were also—and still are—economic. The biggest problem remains the population explosion. When Nasser's father was a boy at the turn of the century, 10 million Egyptians inhabited five million acres. Today the acreage under cultivation has risen to six million, but there are 27 million Egyptians. Each year the population increases by some half a million. The Aswan High Dam, the great project of the revolution, will put another two million acres under the plow, but this addition will be offset by the new Egyptians. Economically Egypt must thus keep running in order to stay in the same place—at least while the economy remains primarily agricultural.

Outside Egypt it is often believed that Nasser's popularity depends on what he is against—particularly Israel and colonialism. In fact, it rests more on the things he is for. One of the most significant of these is industrialization.

THE Arabs are as much in love with factories as the English are with thatched cottages or the Americans with 200-year-old churches. But in Egypt at least, factories can be built only with government participation. For one thing, Middle Eastern capitalists are notorious for insisting on quick returns, which industry rarely gives. As Nasser soon saw, they prefer investing in hotels or office buildings. Also, there is not enough private capital.

Typical of the new men who are making a modern state out of Egypt is the country's minister of industry, Aziz Sidky. At 42, Sidky is well dressed, married and the father of two children; he received his Ph.D. at Harvard in regional economic planning. He is an organization man in the best sense of that term. Under him, industrial investment has grown from a mere six million dollars a year in 1952 to a current rate of almost $600 million.

Sidky believes—as does not only the Arab world but all Asia and Africa—that the reason Asia and Africa are poor is that they are not industrialized. Sidky's own figures seem to bear out his belief.

In 1960 Egypt's agricultural gross product was worth $1.16 billion; in the same year overall industrial production reached a value of three billion dollars. The staggering implication of these statistics is that the 10 million Egyptians engaged in agriculture produce less real wealth than the million or so workers in industry. The only way to produce a standard of living which will begin to compare with that of western countries is to increase agricultural output while simultaneously developing industry.

There are already more than 3,000 factories in Egypt, which each employ more than 25 workers; some of them, like the spinning and weaving mills at Mehalla al Kubra, may employ as many as 25,000 workers. There is eagerness in every town to have a factory; when one is built, telegrams pile up on Sidky's desk from organizations and private individuals in numbers that in the West would greet the star of a successful musical comedy.

How industry can affect a rural community can be shown by one example. Edfu was for long one of the most dispiriting areas in Upper Egypt; except for a 2,000-year-old Ptolemaic temple preserved almost intact in drifting sand, there was nothing worth seeing except the eternal Nile and seedy fields of cotton. The town was a slum. The average profit from an acre was around $20 a year, which gave Edfu one of the lowest per capita incomes in the country. There was the usual disguised unemployment, with far too many men and women on too few fields.

A new factory costing $25 million opened early in 1962. It will use sugar cane, which grows well in the local soil, to produce 20,000 tons of sugar a year. The average yield of an acre will soar to around $180 a year. At the same time, 5,000 workers are employed in the factory itself. With the factory go other benefits: a good school, electricity, piped water and some 500 new housing units. The success of the factory has meanwhile led to the need for a second industry: one which will use the sugarcane pulp to make paper. Nothing else could have turned Edfu so quickly from an embodiment of the hopeless East to a community with hope and purchasing power. The new purchasing power in places like Edfu in turn stimulates industry elsewhere in the country.

Lack of hard currency and lack of skilled manpower are the two major problems which must be overcome before Egypt is able to use industry to turn the country's disaster —its surplus population —into its asset.

Both of these problems are being faced. Foreign assistance to Egypt is considerable. Both the United States and the Soviet Union are committed to contributing amounts in the hundreds of millions of dollars. Yugoslavia is also providing credit, and British, Italian and West German firms are making investments in Egyptian industry. But the need to devote every penny of hard currency to industrialization has annoyed those who remember holidays on the Riviera, when Farouk gambled merrily at the Cannes casino. There is a rigid prohibition on exporting or importing even one Egyptian pound; it is hard for Egyptians to go abroad except on official business or as students.

The problem of skilled manpower can only be met by the leap of faith—by starting. In 1957, when steel was first made at Helwan, near Cairo, with ore mined near Aswan in Upper Egypt, critics alleged that the end product was in fact more expensive than steel obtainable from Europe. To that charge, Aziz Sidky has

HIGH DAM ON THE NILE

Target Date: The Aswan High Dam, located 600 miles south of Cairo, is due for completion in 1967. It will be one of the world's biggest, utilizing some 50 million cubic yards of rock and desert sand to create a 1,544-square-mile artificial lake six times the size of the Hoover Dam's Lake Mead. By 1972 it will bring irrigation to some 1.7 million acres.
Cost: One billion dollars. Russia has pledged to contribute $400 million.
Height: 365 feet, measured from the bed of the Nile. The dam will stretch two and a half miles along its top.
Output: An estimated 10 billion kilowatt-hours a year, about six times the energy being consumed in Egypt.

replied: "For a ton of steel, only a small percentage of the cost is the actual ore mined at Aswan. A large percentage of its price is involved in wages to Egyptian steel workers and transport workers. This is pure gain, since it not only gets money circulating in Egyptian hands which before were empty, but the mills also serve as a technical school for the nation."

Egypt's present ambitions are bound up with the fulfillment of a 10-year development plan inaugurated in 1960 and designed to double the national income by 1970. Egyptians are confident that the plans will be achieved. One of the major goals is the completion of the Aswan High Dam. The biggest single benefit of the dam will be its mammoth production of electricity—enough to bring electricity to the entire Nile Valley.

IT is the presence of this plan, and its execution by men of the caliber of Sidky in industry, Dr. Abdul Moneim al Kaissouny in finance, or Mahmoud Yunis in the administration of the Suez Canal, that makes Egypt different from any other Arab country. This rational attempt to subdue poverty and to bring Egypt into the ranks of modern nations gains Nasser his most potent admirers in other countries of the Arab world.

Nasser's own youthful discovery that Egypt lay at the center of three circles—those enclosing the Arabs, the Moslems and the Africans—has been quoted and requoted. Nasser denies that he wanted to dominate all three. What the young staff officer was stressing was that Egypt could build friendships in these circles and that such friendships could make his country something more than a pawn in the hands of the great powers.

Nasser's efforts to unite the Arab world have in one sense failed, but at the same time he has imposed a way of thinking even on those who attack him most. No Arab leader today openly advocates pro-western policies of the type espoused by the late Nuri Said of Iraq.

Nasser's power is not unlimited, however. His critics note an aspect of Egyptian society which demands change: the immemorial bureaucracy. Soldiers made the 1952 revolution, and they and a gifted group of younger technicians are carrying it out. From them come the fiats and the directives. But these must be filtered through bureaucrats. Not all Egyptian bureaucrats are the kind who hide a desire for cash behind sugary compliments, but enough are to give the image of an Egyptian office an unpleasant tone. "Arab Socialism" requires more office work, not less. Continually the former soldiers and the young technicians issue orders that procedures are to be speeded up—and for a while they are. But the traditions of the bureaucrat need a long time to alter.

The concept of a civil servant is alien to officials who regard the public as both their means of livelihood and *their* servant. Corruption has been abolished at the higher levels, and those who remember the flagrant fortunes made by princes and prime ministers in the old days are thankful for this. But at the small-desk level the under-the-table tip remains. Constant trials for bribery reveal this, as well as the experience of every Egyptian (the bureaucrats are more prudent with foreigners) who has to obtain a document of any shape or size. If Nasser's team can vitalize the bureaucrats, "Arab Socialism" will succeed in Egypt—and having succeeded there, it will attract other Arabs. If the bureaucrats can drown Nasser's Socialism in irritating piles of paper and in commands to "come back tomorrow," Nasserism will fail; Arabs will prefer the inefficiency they know.

EGYPT has greater problems than any other Arab country; it is also attempting to solve them with greater verve. Few ordinary Egyptians complain of a lack of political liberty—though some intellectuals do. Such liberty brought them no benefits under Farouk. To them—so long cut off from power, so long humiliated—it is enough that their dignity is incarnated in the still-youthful president whose words are more than platitudes and whose actions get him, and them, taken seriously by the world outside.

MOUNTAINOUS TOMB of the Pharaoh Khufu rises in majestic dilapidation 451 feet above the desert at Giza. The largest of Egypt's pyramids, it served for many centuries as a convenient stone quarry for local builders.

An Emergence from the Shade of Antiquity

For hundreds of years Egypt stood in the shadow of its own great past. Compared with the ages of the pharaohs and the first caliphs, the centuries that followed were almost one long slide into impotence. As painful evidence of a vanished glory, the ancient structures were largely neglected and occasionally pillaged. Today, in the Egypt of President Gamal Abdul Nasser, the age-old stupor is gone, and ironically enough, antiquity has become the victim of Egypt's revival. When the Aswan High Dam is built, the Nile will threaten many of the greatest ancient monuments. At long last in Egypt, the promising future is putting the awesome past in the shade.

MASSIVE FEET scarred by the names of centuries of tourists are part of four 67-foot-high statues that guard the cave temple of Abu Simbel. Unless salvaged, the huge temple will be submerged beneath a man-made lake.

104

SWAMPED SPHINXES at Wadi es Sebua rest their paws in a seasonal Nile flood. Before the dammed-up Nile engulfs them permanently, they will be put in a museum.

SMUG IMAGES of Ramses II stand 33 feet high at Abu Simbel. To save Abu Simbel's temples, engineers propose to lift them to high ground with hydraulic jacks.

SCHOLARS studying

ancient monuments

now race against time

to finish their work

before many of the relics

are lost forever

PHOTOGRAPHIC RECORD of Abu Simbel is made *(right)* with a copying camera at a documentation center in Cairo. The center has sent an emergency team to record every inch of every relic doomed by the new Aswan dam.

PHARAOH'S VAULT at Thebes *(opposite)* is part of a network of burial chambers in the Valley of the Tombs of Kings. Below this level lies the world-famous tomb of Tutenkhamen, discovered by archeologists in 1922.

ON-THE-SPOT DRAWING of a temple chamber at Wadi es Sebua is executed *(right)* by an architect before the site disappears beneath the Nile. All 25 threatened monuments will be moved or protected, at a cost of $87 million.

WOULD-BE CALIPH of all Islam, King Farouk at 24 still had imperial ambitions and the support of his people.

ROYAL FAMILY assembles *(below)* in 1951 for the wedding of the now-portly Farouk, 31, and Narriman Sadek, 17.

LOUNGING OFFICIALS of King Farouk chat idly alongside Moslem religious leaders in 1950 inside an intricately decorated tent set up for public ceremony. Seated in the imposing gilt chair in the center is the prime minister, Mustafa Nahas, who had been placed in office by the British authorities over the king's futile objections.

TRIUMPHANT REBELS, including General Mohammed Naguib *(center, waving)* and Colonel Gamal Abdul Nasser *(topmost),* are hailed after Farouk's overthrow in 1952.

SPIRITED LEADER, President Nasser sits in his modest study avidly discussing his nation's pivotal position as a leader among the new nations of the Afro-Asian bloc.

A REBIRTH of Egyptian pride and hope came about with the recent rise

to political power of a determined band of progressive-minded young officers

Lined up at a Cairo meeting in 1957, but far from united, are, left to right, Saudi Arabia's King Saud, Syria's President Shukry

Kuwatly, Jordan's King Hussein, Egypt's President Nasser.

Forces for Cohesion and Division

IN every Arab, from Morocco to Kuwait, there is an area of soul which responds to the oratory of Cairo Radio's *Voice of the Arabs:* all Arabs are brothers, and in unity lies strength. Despite the fact that there are many Arab countries, Arabs share a belief that there is an Arab nation whose boundaries override the political frontiers of their states. This force, which is known as *al qawmiyya'l' arabiyya,* or Arab nationalism, is an assertion of dignity and power after the centuries in which Arabs were ruled by foreigners. A force for change, it constitutes the outstanding internal issue in the Arab world. On goals Arabs are largely united, but their individualistic, schismatic natures delight in arguing over the means by which their goals may be attained.

It would be wrong to stigmatize the invocation of Arab nationalism as mere rhetoric. For among all Arabs there is an emotional bond, whether expressed in the correct recitation of the Koran, or among the younger generation in a love for the singers Um Kalthum or Abdul Halim Hafiz. There is also assent to most of Gamal Abdul Nasser's beliefs among the Arab masses, if not their governments, since Nasser's republic remains the magnet of attraction for Arab nationalists. In every Arab city where Egyptian newspapers are allowed, crowds study copies of *al Ahram,* one of the oldest dailies in Egypt. Its editorials by Mohammed Hassanain Haikal represent the developing orthodoxy of Arab nationalism as viewed by Nasser.

THE birth of the United Arab Republic in February 1958 from a fusion of Egypt and Syria showed the force of Arab nationalism. But Syria's secession from the U.A.R. in 1961 showed that drives which make for disunity and schism have their own arguments and their own force. Most opponents of Arab union do not oppose unity, but they argue that complete merger in one superstate is of no advantage to the ordinary Arab.

Some powerful forces for disunion at the moment—the egoism of individual dynasties —will ultimately be the least important. Every cock wishes to stay king of his own barnyard, however limited it may be. No ruler wishes to become ruled. The various Arab kings have a vested interest in separatism.

This has not prevented some kings from toying with Arab nationalism. King Hussein of Jordan, for example, after moving in 1956 to dismiss Lieutenant General John Bagot Glubb as commander of the British-subsidized Arab Legion, was for a while a patriot king in nationalist eyes. He feasted with Nasser in Cairo, and his portrait stood alongside Nasser's in the gossipy, politically minded *souqs,* or bazaars. But Hussein soon realized that the forces which Nasser represented would not preserve a throne founded by Britain. Nasser himself had come to power by throwing out King Farouk, some of whose ancestors had been impressive rulers. Hussein's grandfather, King Abdullah, was assassinated for "treachery," but even so Hussein realized that he could not preserve his throne without relying on western aid, as the

murdered King Abdullah had been forced to do.

King Saud of Saudi Arabia also courted Nasser. To reinforce his own position, he invited the Egyptian president to his country, but was flabbergasted by the popular welcome given in his presence to "the leader of Arabism." For a while, Saud used pictures of himself with Nasser to bolster his own popularity, but he realized that the Socialist tendencies of Nasser could annihilate his expense-account kingdom. A year and a half after the brotherly kissing in Dhahran, Abdul Hamid Serraj, Syria's minister of the interior and Nasser's ally, revealed that he had been offered a seven-figure bribe by the Saudi government to contrive Nasser's death.

The most bizarre client for Nasser's friendship was the Imam of Yemen, a country backward even by comparison with Saudi Arabia. Yet Yemen joined Egypt and Syria in a league called the United Arab States in 1958. This union was one of papyrus, however. Late in 1961 Egypt announced that it had dissolved its association with Yemen since it had led to no reforms inside that country. Continued alliance with the reactionary Imam would have blurred Nasser's image among the Arab masses.

THE one Arab king to have shown significant support for Nasser-style Arab nationalism was the monarch farthest from Cairo, the late Mohammed V of Morocco. He went all the way with Nasser, to the extent of enrolling Morocco in the so-called Casablanca bloc of African states, a group oriented toward Cairo's policies of nonalignment. By continuing this course, his son Hassan II has kept ahead of his own Istiqlal party, which, by invoking nationalist philosophy, could have been a major threat to his rule. But he had other reasons. He is the heir of his father, who was exiled by Morocco's French rulers in 1953 and became a symbol of Arab nationalism. At the same time, Hassan rules a kingdom which even the warlike Turks could not conquer; he has few fears, therefore, of a Nasserist takeover.

Such separate Arab dynasties are immediately the gravest obstacles to Arab unity. They impose the law; they can punish those who advocate Arab unity by sentences ranging from the barbarous to the sophisticated. At the same time, these obstacles are not likely to last forever. There is hardly an Arab dynasty which is rooted in the affections of the people it rules, in the sense in which the Bernadotte dynasty is popular in Sweden, let alone the royal family in Britain.

Not all distrust of Egypt and its doctrine of Arab nationalism is based on the reluctance of a king to lose his crown or the fear of a president that he will be demoted. There are obstacles to Arab unity which are likely to be longer lasting and more troublesome than personal egoism. Throughout the Arab world, there are local particularisms of varying force which Arab unity would threaten. These are basically of two kinds: religious and racial.

Lebanon provides the best example of a religious minority apprehensive of Arab unity. The Lebanese are proud of having the highest literacy rate and standard of living in the Arab world. The Maronite Christian element has to a great extent imposed its pattern on the country's society, but even the Maronite Patriarch has stated that the Christians are now probably in a minority. In the exercise of power, they are, nevertheless, an effective majority. The Lebanese Christians (or a majority of them) are determined not to join an Arab union in which they would become a tiny fraction.

A LEBANESE Christian who exemplifies this determination is Raymond Eddé, a lawyer and one of the most lucid brains in the Middle East. His father, Emile Eddé, was the pro-French President of Lebanon under the French mandate; the younger Eddé himself was minister of the interior after the troubles of 1958 in which supporters of President Camille Chamoun, admirers of Gamal Abdul Nasser and special-interest groups fought each other throughout Lebanon. "I am against any form of Arab union, federal or otherwise," Raymond Eddé says. "Collaboration, yes; total agreement over Israel, yes; but union, definitely no." His opposition is not only to those forms of Arab union advocated by Nasser. In January 1962 he played a leading role in suppressing the abortive coup which was led by the Syrian Popular party, an anti-Egyptian group aiming at a united "Fertile Crescent" of Lebanon, Syria, Iraq and Jordan.

S IMILARLY, sectional impulses pull Iraq away from union with other Arab states. Iraq is Egypt's chief rival in wealth and influence in the Arab world, a position which may be challenged by independent Algeria. Yet it is doubtful that Iraqi nationalism exists in a positive sense, although the British tried to foster a feeling of national identity when the state came into existence after World War I.

More than half the Iraqi Arabs are Shiites, members of an ancient and sometimes persecuted Moslem sect whose creed is the state religion in Iraq's neighbor Iran. Two of the Shiite holy cities are in Iraq; the Shiites are found chiefly in the southern, poorer part of the country. The Shiites' quarrel with other Moslems is an ancient one: they believe that on Mohammed's death the leadership of Islam should have passed to Ali, his son-in-law, and they trace a series of Imams through Ali's descendants by Fatima, the Prophet's daughter. The Shiites believe that in the future a messiah figure will return to lead Islam. Few young Iraqis pay attention to these beliefs. But under the orthodox Moslem Turks the Shiites were oppressed, and to this day there is in Iraq a residue of suspicion against orthodox Moslems such as the Egyptians. In an Arab union the Shiites, like the Lebanese Christians, would become less important than they are at present.

There is also a sizable racial minority in Iraq which is suspicious of Arab unity. The Kurds are energetic, tough, honest mountaineers who speak an Indo-European language akin to Persian. By religion they are Sunni Moslems like most Arabs. Their difficulty, as a would-be nation, is that they are dispersed throughout a number of countries—Turkey, Iran, Iraq, Syria and the U.S.S.R.—and their area lacks natural boundaries. In Iraq they compose about a quarter of the population. The climate of their hills is more severe than that of lowland Iraq, and they are robust soldiers. In the pre-1958 Iraq of Prime Minister Nuri Said they played an important role; their role in present-day Iraq has been ambiguous. Premier Abdul Karim Kassem has used them against the partisans of unity under Nasser, and he explicitly named the new Iraqi state "a union of Arabs and Kurds." But he has been unable to integrate them fully into the state. Armed clashes between Kurdish mountaineers and government troops have been frequent.

The Kurds are not Communists. But in their struggle to maintain their national identity they have used (and have been used by) the Russians. They are proud of the fact that the greatest "Arab" leader at the time of the Crusades, Saladin, was in fact a Kurd. But they fear that if they contributed their support to a modern Arab union, they might be swallowed up in an intransigent Arabism. Their present ambitions are to have more money spent on their villages, to obtain a measure of autonomy and to have Kurdish culture protected by the state. In Turkey they have been disposed of as "mountain Turks"; they fear that similar cultural suppression might be their fate in an Arab union.

BECAUSE the Arab world is in reality only "Arabized" and not "Arab," submerged groups can be discovered in every part of it. The Berbers of North Africa constituted the native population under the Roman-Byzantine domination of the area. Suffering from Roman oppression and from Christian sectarian strife, they were rapidly converted to Islam. But the Berbers have maintained their language and their identity. The Nilotic people of the Sudan owe their religion and their language to Arab conquerors; they admire, but also suspect, their northern neighbors. Egypt itself, a country of villages, has its own form of particularism.

The same is true of Palestinians, Moroccans and Tunisians. President Habib Bourguiba of Tunisia was a political refugee in Faroukian Egypt. Yet he wrote from Cairo in 1948: "No, I refuse to break with the past. . . . For my soul is always in Tunisia, waiting for the day when my body will rejoin it there." If the roles had been reversed and Nasser had been an exile in Tunis, the pull of the Nile Valley would have been just as strong.

THE Arab world is so vast and the communication within it until recently so bad that it is not surprising that provincialism tugs against unity. Arab nationalists believe that these local emotions need be no stronger than the loyalty which Texans feel for their sovereign state, or Rhinelanders for their vinous valley.

The strengths and weaknesses of Arab nationalism have been tested under laboratory conditions. For between 1958 and 1962, there was the spotlit quarrel of centripetal and centrifugal forces in Syria.

Geographically, Syria has little logical entity. Its steppes merge imperceptibly with those of Iraq and Jordan; for centuries Syria was a term that included Palestine and Lebanon. The Syrian Arabs have always remembered that the first imperial caliphate was based at Damascus; the Syrian constitution of 1950 explicitly stated that Syria was "part of the Arab nation."

In the winter of 1957-1958, Syria was encircled by problems. The Communist party was gaining ground, and this frightened the strong middle-class element of Damascus and Aleppo. The United States Secretary of State, John Foster Dulles, expressed ominous concern; troops massed on both sides of the Turkish border; Syria and Egypt accused Iraq's King Feisal and his cousin Hussein of Jordan of intrigues against Syria; the army was guarding the Israeli front. The country's established politicians, from President Shukry Kuwatly down, had always advocated Arab union. In this emergency, the Syrian leaders flew to Cairo and presented Nasser with what amounted to an ultimatum: total union, or Syria would be lost.

Nasser was in a dilemma. He, too, had made Arab unity a major article of his creed; at home he had discerned the danger of Communism and done all in his power to suppress it. At the same time, he was aware of the difficulties which union would involve. Every Syrian was a politician, the commercially minded Syrians were unlike the agricultural Egyptians, and there was no tradition in Syria of strong central government. Above all, the presence of Israel made wheeled traffic between the two countries impossible.

But to save Syria from Communism, and at the same time to rebuff the "colonialism" which, like every Arab nationalist, he saw lurking everywhere, Nasser accepted the ultimatum. On February 1, 1958, the United Arab Republic came into being. The union was overwhelmingly endorsed by what now came to be known as "the two regions of the U.A.R." Crowds chanted a new song: "I am Egyptian and you are Syrian, I am Syrian and you are Egyptian."

Yet hardly had the radios cooled down when the union began to creak. It was not possible to employ all the politicians who had flown from Damascus to Cairo; those without jobs began to regret their altruism. Communism was quickly defeated in Syria by police action and a radical program that had more appeal to the Moslem masses; the rich were no longer as frightened of popular revenge as before. The outside world accepted the union without protest; the fear of attack receded, and Syrian officers began to think in terms of promotion rather than patriotic mission. Gradually the same laws were applied in the two regions. These included laws limiting landholdings and others designed to improve the lot of the workers, and these enactments were by no means to the taste of the Syrian commercial classes.

THE final crisis developed in July 1961, when Nasser announced new decrees designed to achieve "Arab Socialism." The Egyptian president was aware of what western journalists had long been writing: while his political revolution had succeeded, most of his people remained poor. The Socialist laws were not popular with the remnants of Egypt's own wealthy class, but they no longer had decisive importance.

In Syria, the rich were far more powerful. Syrian farmers were often entrepreneurs, making large sums from cash crops. Unluckily, the three summers of union saw a drought. Rich Syrians had always gone to Beirut to have a good time; the new Socialist controls and restrictions on travel seemed the last straw.

THUS, by the autumn of 1961 there was a sufficient undercurrent of discontent in Syria to support a successful military coup whose leaders severed relations with Egypt. Egyptian officials in Syria had not always been polite or efficient; those who had been both suffered along with the rest from a resurgence of provincial separatism. Many Syrians had come to feel that their country had been turned into a protectorate.

The army coup claimed to be restoring civilian, constitutional rule. Cairo claimed that it was a reactionary move, planned by those whose interests lay in oppressing the fellahin and the industrial workers. Curiously enough, six months later—after a new president, cabinet and parliament had all been elected—the military repeated its intervention, abolished this democratic apparatus and published statements repeating word for word the Cairo charges.

The union of Syria and Egypt had been greeted with joy by Arab nationalists; the dissolution brought a far different reaction. Such a practical businessman as Emile Bustani of Lebanon, who was in the United States when the news came, admits to having wept in his hotel bedroom when he heard of the Syrian secession. At the same time, the double experience reminded Arabs everywhere that there was a difference between words and reality. To construct union would mean sacrifices, not merely euphoric songs and dancing in the streets. When the music stopped, the challenges remained.

Most observers agreed that the U.A.R. had done much for Syria. It had saved the country from a series of tragic coups; it had brought teachers where none had been before. But there was no democratic organization to defend these "social gains." The Syrian members of Nasser's one-party political organization, the National Union, were a gang of opportunist yes men, who voted "no" as soon as the military told them to. The "social gains" were fiats from Cairo, emanating from a president genuinely loved, but carried out by officials nearly always distrusted. The Socialist laws were in no sense the results of popular discussion; they had not even been submitted to the National Union; and when the coup came, there was no way in which the people could show what they desired. In the elections that followed, however, less than 40 per cent of the people cast a vote, hinting that the dissolution of the union was not really popular.

Probably most people were divided. They wanted union for emotional reasons. They wanted social reforms, to the degree in which these benefited themselves. But they suffered rather than benefited from the extension of the bureaucratic apparatus. This applied to Egyptians as much as Syrians. The Egyptians were sad at the breakup of the union, because Nasser was sad. For themselves, many were secretly glad. It had always been hard to get things done in government offices. With the bureaucracy straddling between Egypt and Syria, things were getting worse. President Nasser himself said that Syria had taken up three quarters of his time. Until Arab bureaucracy becomes smooth, honest and swift, ordinary Arabs will probably prefer the smaller unit, where at least they know the ropes, to the larger, where individual contacts mean far less.

THE present period is one of great debate for Arabs. Although they agree on their objective, they have seen the collapse of the first serious attempt to realize unity. They are re-examining what they desire and how they intend to achieve it. At one extreme, there are those who assert that more money can be made and a better existence achieved for the ordinary Arab if no union comes about at all. These arguments have force in such countries as Lebanon or Kuwait, where there is a high standard of living already and where geography and natural resources combine to produce capital.

At the other extreme, nationalists point out that countries like the United States are prosperous precisely because they are large and united: where would American prosperity be, they ask, if there were customs posts at every state frontier and if a businessman needed a visa to go from Massachusetts to Manhattan? And behind these economic motives for Arab unity lies the deeper impulse of an emotional fervor: if only the Arabs founded one great superstate they would be more respected in the world. They would have more power.

BOTH points of view can be reconciled. The first attempt at union was far too extreme. The effort had been made to scramble two diverse countries, Egypt and Syria, in a total unity similar to that of the United States. But while the United States had been created in the 18th Century, when the realm of government was smaller, Syria and Egypt had at once embarked on a most complicated social change. Social engineering anywhere requires a tactful bureaucracy; to effect it smoothly in two hastily married states needs the service of angels.

It would be far more sensible, most Arabs now agree, if union remained the goal, but on a federal basis. This would give the economic boost which stimulates industrial growth; at the same time it would permit the component parts of the Arab world to move at their own pace in their own way.

To achieve such a system is the new challenge. History will show whether it will be met. Perhaps Syria will rejoin the U.A.R., this time on a federal basis; perhaps this same federal system will at last allow Iraq and Egypt to work in one harness, neither feeling pulled by the other. Perhaps regional mergers will take place: a federation of North Africa, another of the Nile Valley, another of the Middle East.

But whatever happens, the forces for union will remain. So will the forces for disunion. For some time to come Arabs will be able to parody St. Augustine's prayer with the words, "Make us united—but not yet."

The articles of union between Syria and Egypt are signed by Presidents Kuwatly and Nasser in 1958. The union dissolved in 1961.

A Divided Family's Painful Rivalries

A sense of potential unity is a major cause of the political rivalries that rend the Arab world. The ideal of an "Arab nation" is strong, and actual political boundaries are considered to be temporary partitions. Because a leader of one state might win the loyalty of all Arabs, no government is really safe. A surge of Arab unity might transform a royal realm into a minor province. In the Arab world, therefore, political maneuvering is often a matter of life or death.

WITH MODERATE President Camille Chamoun of Lebanon, sharply reactionary King Saud of Arabia meets in 1957 to stress the territorial integrity of the Arab states.

WITH ANTI-NASSERITE Premier Nuri Said of Iraq, King Saud tries to cement an alliance against Egypt's president, whose progressivism threatened their monarchies.

WITH PRO-NASSERITE President Kuwatly of Syria *(opposite)*, King Saud meets in Damascus during his 1957 visit in an attempt to draw Syria out of Egypt's orbit.

WITH ROYAL COLLEAGUE King Hussein of Jordan, King Saud observes perfect protocol in befriending a man whose family has feuded with Saud's for decades.

STABILITY in Morocco has been upset by the unsettled state of North Africa, forcing a conservative monarchy to plunge into tricky political waters

ROYAL PARDON is granted to a groveling Berber chief by Morocco's late ruler, Mohammed Ben Youssef, on the latter's return from exile in 1955. The chief, the Pasha of Marrakesh, had pleaded for the royal forgiveness for conniving with France to overthrow Mohammed in 1953.

PRAYING SUBJECTS mourn with the royal family *(foreground)* at the funeral of King Mohammed in 1961, held at the ruins of a 12th Century mosque in Rabat. The Alaouite Dynasty has reigned in Morocco for three centuries, but from 1912 to 1956 France was in control.

WILY SUCCESSOR to his father, King Hassan II is an absolute monarch, but he is sharply opposed by powerful left-wing groups. To demonstrate his adherence to progressive movements, Hassan has ostentatiously supported Algeria's firebrand Arab nationalists, although they have little sympathy for his traditionalist regime.

MEDINA'S EDGE, an entrance to the old Arab quarter of Tunis leads to a dense district of winding streets and arcaded mosques. Nearby, the French, who governed Tunisia from 1881 to 1956, built their own Paris-like quarter. Despite Tunisian hostility to French rule, young Tunisians have retained strong cultural ties with France.

MODERATION is the policy of a Tunisian leader who dares to be pro-western

TEMPERATE HERO, Habib Bourguiba returns to Tunisia in 1955 after winning French recognition of Tunisia's rights to self-government. Now president, he is opposed to the fanatic elements among Arab nationalists.

DIPLOMATIC REFORMER, President Bourguiba calls on the Bey of Tunis in 1957. Later that year Tunisia was declared a republic and the bey, a figurehead ruler, was deposed, ending a dynasty that had lasted 252 years.

Attentive engineers gather to watch a demonstration in the machine shop of Cairo University's busy school of engineering. A serious

An Acceptance of Change

dearth of trained technicians exists in all the Arab countries.

IN 1908 Britain's Earl of Cromer, summing up his administration in Egypt, quoted with sympathy a fellow countryman's dictum that an educated Moslem must be either "a fanatic or a concealed infidel." To many outsiders besides Cromer it seemed that a modern Moslem was a contradiction in terms. Either a man would be a Moslem, and thus a reactionary, or he would be modern-minded and break with Islam. One of the surprises of the 20th Century has been the way the Arab Moslems have accepted change and the modern world. They have done this with revolutionary speed, yet without making that radical break with the religious past that characterized Communist Russia or the Turkey of Kemal Ataturk.

This acceptance of change has not yet spread to Saudi Arabia and Yemen, though even in these Zealot kingdoms there are currents for reform. Everywhere else Arab modernism is a tangible, visible, audible force. Change may roll its strongest tides over Lebanon and Egypt, but with oceanic power the waves wash everywhere else, too.

In nothing is this fundamental movement of change more evident than in the position of women. Modern Arabs claim with some justification that the subjugation of women was not original with Islam. The Greek dramatist Euripides wrote that a woman had no honor outside the house. Arabs also point out that an important part in early Islam was played not only by businesswomen like Khadija, who supported Mohammed when no one else did, but also by women soldiers who rode beside the conquering Moslem warriors.

Nor were women particularly subservient to men during Islam's earliest centuries. Sukayna, a great-granddaughter of the Prophet, kept a literary salon in Medina. She had a taste for practical jokes, once making an old sheik sit on a basket of eggs and cluck to amuse her guests. A niece of the Prophet's wife Ayesha was scolded by her husband for not veiling her face. "Since God has stamped me with beauty," she replied, "it is my wish that the public should view that beauty and thereby recognize His grace unto them. Under no conditions, therefore, will I veil myself."

DESPITE those stories, there is no denying that after the middle of the Eighth Century upper-class Islamic society suffered from a prevalence of harems. While the harem system and the ancient Semitic custom of veiling never caught on in the countryside, where the women worked beside the men, in urban Arab communities the veil was for many centuries part of every woman's experience.

The word harem derives from the word *haram*, which means forbidden or sacred. Women were long regarded within the Arab world as private, not to be visited by men outside the family circle. The harem system is sometimes defended as having arisen in times of war, when women needed protection. In fact, it meant their being considered instruments of a man's pleasure and the bearers of his children. Psychologically the institution of the guarded harem was linked not only with a distrust of women but also with an obsession for safeguarding paternity. The only way in which a man could feel completely certain that a child was his own was by placing an inordinate value first on virginity in his bride and then on the seclusion of his wife. A girl who was not a virgin at marriage would always be returned to her own family, in whose fraternal ranks she was quite likely to be slain to avenge the family honor. The monstrous invention of eunuchs as guards for princely enclosures was a logical corollary of this attitude. There is no justification for eunuchs or harems in the Koran, which merely stresses that women should be modest and that men (who have to support them) are in charge of them.

The harem and its psychological pillars have been dynamited by the 20th Century. In Europe the emancipation of women came slowly. In the Arab world it has come like an avalanche. In some European and American universities, women first won the right to study literature and only later the less modest subject of medicine. In Baghdad young women stepped from shuttered houses into the dissecting rooms. Today in Cairo women from the Ministry of Social Affairs pry into the conditions of labor; burly garage owners quail before their questions. In a country such as Egypt, multitudes of women engage in teaching, and in every other aspect of life women play an increasing part. There are women lawyers, surgeons, engineers and accountants. Women are doing cosmic ray research. Women journalists send copy from London, Delhi and Peking.

MEN still believe that a family's honor resides in the chastity of its women. What a man's sister does with her spare time is very much his business. In economic affairs, however, women are almost men's equals. In general, they are paid the same rate for the same job, and Moslem women, only too conscious of their suppression in the past, will plead what is true—that for 13 centuries they have had one important advantage over their western sisters:

control over their own assets. In Britain, it was not until the passage in 1882 of the Married Women's Property Act that an Englishwoman's estate became safe from marital schemers. Moslem women have always retained their property on getting married; this was their safeguard against divorce, which in Islam was very simple. A man had only to say three times the words "I divorce you," and the marriage was at an end. But in such circumstances the woman retained the money and property she had brought with her as well as the dowry that had been settled on her by her husband.

A major argument of those who have urged the emancipation of women has been the impossibility of fostering education when the mothers of the new generation are themselves uneducated. In the Arab world, education of girls as well as boys has taken a fantastic leap forward in the last two decades. In one Arab country alone, Egypt, there are now a million more children in primary school than there are people in Israel. In Morocco, 5,300 girls attended school in 1939, and 20 years later the number had soared to 180,000.

STRONGER ROLE for women is satirized in a Cairo cartoon. "Elect me," the wife is saying. "I will know how to defend women's rights."

The new attitude toward women is fundamental in its motivation and in its effects. The previous attitude was linked to two historic facts of Arab life: first, the suppression of the ordinary Arab, originally by Moslem rulers and then by European imperialists, and second, a compensatory exaggeration of the father image. The powerless fellah or the hardly more powerful townsman could be beaten or imprisoned, conscripted or despoiled without recourse. At the same time, in a desperate move to bolster his own ego, he made himself a tyrant within the four walls of his home. Lack of freedom for the man outside the household led to lack of freedom for the women inside it.

The departure of the imperialists and the attainment of self-government by nearly all of the Arab states have led to a new self-confidence. The foreigner is now far more welcome than in the days when the countries he visited were administered by his countrymen. Englishmen who remember surly faces in Egypt have been astonished by the smiles received in modern Cairo. This new self-confidence reflects itself internally in a downgrading of the father image. The Arab father is still far from being a Dagwood. But he is no longer an absolute monarch.

A new permissiveness has spread from the once-authoritarian homes to the outer world of communications and the arts in general. As Princess Lalla Ayesha, a sister of King Hassan II of Morocco, is seen in nurse's uniform after an earthquake, as Nasser's daughter is photographed leading a procession of girl bicyclists through Cairo, so a new phenomenon—pictures painted by the students —marks the walls of schools from one end of the Arab world to another.

The visual arts were long restricted among Arabs by a taboo on the representation of the human form. The taboo was never absolute. It was defied in Egypt from the 10th through the 12th Century by the Fatimid Dynasty, whose pottery showed turbaned musicians with their lutes. Despite such ceramics, and others from Samarra in Iraq, orthodox Moslems generally disapproved of the portrayal of saints or even ordinary men and women in painting or sculpture. Like Jews, Moslems felt that such representation was the first step toward idolatry. The strong esthetic impulses of the Moslems were forced into intricate arabesques—formalized patterns of color and shape.

In the 20th Century this taboo against representing nature has dissolved. The Arab artist is no longer confined to calligraphy or the decorative arts. From Morocco to Iraq, there is vast enthusiasm for painting and sculpture. The teaching of art in the schools leads to an appreciation of more sophisticated forms when school days are past. Inevitably, when a country with little traditional skill in painting takes up the art, difficulties arise. Either the painting imitates what is current abroad, or it goes back in a conscious search to its own millennial past.

THIS is true of much modern Arab painting. While Arab children paint with the freshness and impetus remarkable in children everywhere, adult Arab artists often wander haphazardly in the morasses of modern art or play with the forms invented by ancestral Egyptians and Babylonians. Sure-fingered in calligraphy and their own decorative tradition, Arabs are often awkward when they work in an art that was not previously their own. The same is true with those members of the new middle class who buy pictures. Calendar art (Capri at sunset with girl dangling cherries over half-opened mouth) sells well. Also popular is sentimental neorealistic painting with a message.

Parallel with these evidences of failure are the works of artists of vision and integrity. Numerous exhibitions are held in Cairo throughout the year. Nothing shows the persistent cosmopolitanism of Cairo better than the names of the artists who exhibit; the works of Arabs, Armenians, Italians, Hungarians and Greeks are all on display. Women (Tahia Halim, to mention only one) are prominent. While the Egyptian painter Mahmoud Said has the lush talents of a first-class magazine illustrator, Iraq's Jewad Saleem, who died in 1961 at the age of 41, not only achieved international success but was the only Middle East artist to win an award in the worldwide 1952 competition for a memorial to the Unknown Political Prisoner. Saleem was commissioned by Iraq to design a monument

to commemorate its 1958 revolution. The completed monument is grandiose, original and completely of this century. Its strident angular figures boldly parade against a bare wall that forms an end of the largest square in Baghdad.

If change is putting paintbrushes into hands unused to them, change is also affecting the Arabs' immemorial obsession with words. Poetry was always the art in which Arabs excelled. And modern Arabs are recovering a power which over uncreative centuries had been wasted on the verbal equivalent of rococo.

Iraq, for example, was fertile in poets in the centuries after Mohammed, and today it again excels in the production of poets and in the appreciation of them. The loveliest street in Baghdad—the boulevard by the river Tigris where little cafés glitter at night and fishermen grill fish staked around a fire—is named after Abu Newas, the debauched poet who lived at the same time as Haroun al Rashid, the Caliph of Baghdad from 786 to 809 A.D. College gatherings, social occasions and political meetings are all improved for Iraqis if they are embellished by poetry.

EGYPT has done most with prose. From 1800 on, there has been a fascinating development from verbosity through contrived elegance to a contemporary style which can, in expert hands, be expressive, unpedantic and even concise.

The senior Egyptian writer is Taha Hussein, blind, old and immensely respected. He was a village boy who studied at al Azhar, the 1,000-year-old Islamic university in Cairo. His account of his school years, *The Days*, has become a modern classic.

Towfik al Hakim, younger than Taha Hussein, comes nearer to being a cosmopolitan writer than anyone writing in modern Arabic. However good contemporary Arab writers are, they usually tend to illustrate Arab themes, not the universal condition of man. There is thus something provincial in all Arab writing. In its favor, a critic could argue that through a close study of Egyptian life in a crowded Cairo street or a delta village, universal man is described, not merely Arab man. But the playwright and novelist Towfik al Hakim is perhaps the only writer who has deliberately attempted to relate Arabs to humanity in general. One of his novels, *Sparrow from the East,* puts an Arab student in close touch with people in Paris. There is a scene of remarkable insight in which the Arab hears the dying words of a Russian anticommunist exile. The Russian wants to spend his remaining francs on a ticket to the Middle East, there to escape into the last citadel of the romantic world. The Arab recognizes that this is illusion: in his homeland, too, men are in love with factories and power.

THE best novelist that Egypt has produced is Naguib Mahfouz. Now middle-aged, Mahfouz has been spinning over the years a series of detailed tapestries describing the milieu he knows best, that of the back streets of Cairo. Titles like *Khan al Khalili,* the name of the goldsmiths' bazaar, indicate his region. Mahfouz is a realist, and yet one of the major problems of modern Arabic baffles him. Every Arab writer who aspires to realism must confront the problem: in what language should his characters converse? In reality, people almost never talk classical Arabic, but in print the colloquial tongue offends readers. Mahfouz makes his working-class characters converse in classical Arabic. The problem was solved differently by Abdul Rahman Sharkawi in his novel *Egyptian Earth,* where the author makes his characters speak as they really do—not merely in colloquial Egyptian but in the particular dialect of one area of the Nile Delta. He thus gains in realism, although he loses in the power to please pedants.

Two writers enjoy a vogue among the young comparable to that of Françoise Sagan in France —Ihsan Abdul Kaddous and Yusif al Sebai. Kaddous writes immense novels about the more cosmopolitan layers in Egyptian society, but he is at his best in his short stories. His critics find him shallow—but shallow water sometimes flows clearer than deep, and Kaddous is never dull. His novel *A Man in Our House* describes a politically minded student who kills a cabinet minister and then takes refuge with a middle-class Cairo family. The confined world, the idealism of the student warring with his attachment for a daughter of the house are not merely documentary. The quality of tension would not be scorned by a Hemingway.

Yusif al Sebai, one of the officers involved in the 1952 revolution, is the nearest to a "Nasserist" novelist to be found. His book *Return, My Heart* was made into a film which for color, sweep and melodrama might be called the Egyptian *Gone with the Wind.* It tells the story of a gardener's son who idealizes the pasha's daughter, becomes an army officer, fights in Palestine, loves a bad girl, gains the love of the pasha's daughter and in the last scene dispossesses her arrogant brother of his excess acres. One scene shows the officers swearing on the Koran the oath to liberate Egypt; when the picture was shown in Arab cities, people jumped on their seats with enthusiasm.

THESE modern Egyptian writers give a close picture of Egyptian society, but they rarely delve very deeply into human motivation, and not one of them has begun to write about sexual love with anything of the penetration shown by the anonymous composers of the classic *Thousand and One Nights.* This magical compilation of fairy stories and baroque adventures shows the Arab imagination at its most vivid. The structure is given by the beautiful Shahrazad's scheme to avoid death by keeping the ruler so interested in what will happen next in her stories that he continually postpones his threat to murder her (he has slain all her predecessors) until the next night; after 1,001 such nights he takes pity on her and spares her.

The Thousand and One Nights not only shows the power which a woman could wield by her wits over the master of her world, but also provides a folk portrait of the realm of Haroun al Rashid. The descriptions of love have a candor which even D. H. Lawrence, the author of *Lady Chatterley's Lover,* never achieved. Yet in Cairo the popular editions of *The Thousand and One Nights* have all been bowdlerized, for puritanism is also a factor in the spirit of the new Arab world.

This puritanism is shown not only in regulations which compel a belly dancer to cover her midriff but also in the most popular of all Arab arts—the cinema. Movie houses are packed throughout the Arab world, and Egypt in some years has produced more than 70 films. The censor rules over the films with capricious rod. Scenes which would be cut from European or American movies are left intact, but scenes which in the West would have no prurient meaning are prudishly removed.

There is little realism so far in Egyptian movies. The average middle-class saga is set in a modest home modeled on one of King Farouk's former residences; heroes have private airplanes; the sorrows of life are smoothed away by money. This may, or so the producers argue, appeal to people whose lives are for the most part set apart from comfort. Only a few directors have broken through to poetry and realism. One is Yusif Shaheen. Trained in California, he produced a film called *Bab al Hadeed,* the name of the Cairo railroad station. The film is a study in schizophrenia, unburdened by false attitudes. Kinawi, a crippled waif, sells newspapers on the station platforms. He falls in love with a bawdy wench who takes from him his only treasure, a gold ornament that belonged to his mother, and then mocks him and his limping gait with a cruel laugh. Obsessed, the cripple subsides into the character of a sex-murderer whose headlined crimes he has shouted to the passengers on the platform. He becomes the villain and kills not his beloved but another girl.

I N *Bab al Hadeed,* Shaheen reaches out of the Arab province and shows, in his unfortunate victim-hero, the tragedy of all those who suffer from some inborn defect or deviation. He also shows something of the Arab character, capable of switching from generosity to violence if rebuffed or ill-used. When the picture was chosen in 1962 to represent Egypt at an American film festival, there were protests from Arab students in West Germany (where *Bab al Hadeed* was also being shown) that it showed the Arabs in a backward and unfavorable light. In fact, it universalizes compassion; for photography and direction it has hardly been equaled in the Arab world.

Television, as in other parts of the world, is a new rival to motion pictures. Already many Arab stations are busy projecting television's chaotic yet stimulating image of the 20th Century. Iraq was the first Arab state to introduce television, back in 1956, but Egypt now leads in volume and quality. As elsewhere in the world, purists would restrict the first and improve the second.

ALTHOUGH so far there are only 150,000 sets, the number constantly grows; a new factory is producing cheap sets. Already many cafés and public squares are equipped. Demure belly dances, newsreels, patriotic dramas, the lengthy recitals of the singer Um Kalthum, English and Arabic lessons, adventure programs from the United States, speeches by Nasser—a weird medley imposes itself on people who in the past were restricted to one narrow cultural alley, walled perhaps by an Islamic mosque, striking in its beauty, yet as out of date as the 14th Century in which it was constructed.

Dr. Abdul Kader Hatem, the energetic Egyptian minister responsible for television, believes in the positive role that it can play in building a modern Arab consciousness. Certainly the impact of the outside world is dramatic and direct, and throughout Egypt, in the vast square outside the Nile Hilton in Cairo, or in delta townlets, men and women fix their eyes on the small screen.

In a sense, the quantitative impact of movies and television is having a greater effect on the Arab consciousness than the studied pleas for change advanced over the last century or more by Moslem reformers. For the modern world infuses its own standards without argument, and they are, in this way, unarguable.

Nasser, who is in a sense heir of the earlier reformers, appeals to his people to recognize that work is the only road to prosperity. The pictorialized images of the outside world seen by the Arab millions are as potent as his words. In that world a different attitude toward work exists. In the past, work was despised. Just as the big belly was long a sign that a man had more than enough to eat, so a neat western suit became a sign that a young man had arrived— he had taken his college degree, had become a bureaucrat and henceforward would give orders: "Bring a coffee, extra sweet" or to some defenseless citizen, "Come back tomorrow." Not long ago every ambitious boy wished to be a bey, the Turkish term for sir. Even now servile echoes of the past whisper in government ministries, where hordes of bureaucrats pour their malice on the public and their servility on their superiors: "The bey's happiness is in Alexandria" is the way they might state the mundane fact that "the boss is out of town."

THIS old ideal of educated youth (an office, a white collar, a cup of coffee and at least one telephone) is under siege. A new generation has begun to run, not strut. Sport is a mania among Arab youths, who are good at boxing, soccer, swimming and basketball. Sport, in fact, is to the new generation what politics was to Nasser's generation. Cairo and Beirut, to name only two Arab capitals, have impressive stadiums; the one in Cairo is the largest in Africa and the Middle East. A slum area of Cairo was until recently given over to sprawling rubbish dumps larger than city blocks; in caves women sold hashish and themselves to any who came. Now the whole area has been leveled and a sports center opened for the city's youth. There are football fields, a parachute tower, a track field and a gymnasium.

In all Arab countries the new mood derives from the young. It is much more difficult to modernize an old society from within than to construct a totally new society in a new land; the old people and their attitudes are like absorbent cotton that muffles the will to shout or to attack. But the pressure of youth is beginning to achieve such a change nevertheless.

Young engineers are working in the "new valley" in Egypt's Western Desert; significantly, there is a new interest in adventure for its own sake. A successful book has been published by a student who hitchhiked around Egypt, through deserts and oases, covering a distance of 3,555 miles. He had originally planned to hitchhike abroad, following the Riviera route known to wealthy Egyptians of the pre-Nasser period. It was suggested that he might first get to know his own land. He responded, and others are following in his tracks.

Change is the greatest unifying factor in the new Arab world, for all Arab youth share a sense of belonging to a generation which has the power to remake their world. The feuds and dynastic quarrels which divided their fathers mean little to young Arabs. Iraqis, to cite only one case, now get indignant if asked to which Islamic sect they belong; such preoccupations have little meaning to them. In their eyes, whatever modernizes the Arab world is good; whatever holds it back is bad.

Hence the eagerness with which visitors to the Arab world will be shown hospitals, factories, schools; hence the sometimes amazing indifference to precious antiquities shown by those who have grown up with them. Western visitors to Cairo or Baghdad buy postcards of the Sphinx or the Gate of Babylon. The Egyptian or Iraqi on tour hunts for pictures of a new hotel, a television station or a steel mill. Such gestures, extolling change, unite the young Arab of Iraq with the young Arab of Egypt.

FOR long the Arabs felt themselves prisoners of a mold. They are now breaking free. Their struggles may be gauche and their mistakes big, but they are determined, from Morocco to Iraq, to destroy the old stereotypes. The new stereotypes may not please the tourist who craves the picturesque, or the antiquarian who worships the old. But they please the Arabs, who are burning their fezzes and their whole apparatus of traditional dress. In assuming as their own the costumes and customs of the West, they show what they admire.

A Newly Sharpened Taste for the New

Although modern factories are relatively few in the Arab world, the very desire to acquire them constitutes a revolutionary force. A passion for industrialism is the centerpiece of the new idealism. Arab nationalism is viewed by many as the power that comes from developing an industrial economy. By existing simply as an ideal, industrialism is accomplishing swiftly what a century of direct European influence had failed to do—make the ways of the West seem admirable to large numbers of Arabs. It has lent prestige to science and technology. In all fields it has sharpened a taste for the new and the experimental. The very desire for change will in the long run be the most potent force for reform in the changing Arab world.

GYMNASTS at a privately owned textile plant in Egypt wrestle on a broad canvas apron provided by the management for off-hour recreation. The company also furnishes its employees with housing and vocational training.

SPOOLED COTTON is wheeled on a rack through the grounds of the Mehalla al Kubra textile factory near Cairo. Textile manufacturing, which has increased considerably in the past decade, is Egypt's largest industry.

FASTIDIOUS BREAK is taken by five Moroccans who keep up the time-honored ritual of coffee-drinking on a factory rooftop in Casablanca. Beyond are the plants which process the country's mineral wealth for export.

Rising to sing in the classic quavering Arab style, middle-aged Um

ROYAL FEMINIST in trim dress and high-heeled shoes, Princess Ayesha, sister of Morocco's King Hassan II, is a leading advocate of freedom for Arab women.

EMANCIPATED WOMEN who lead public lives and wear western clothes are no longer rare as the custom of female seclusion dies out

Kàlthum performs in Cairo before some of her millions of admirers.

SUCCESSFUL ARTIST, Aida Marini is one of the most accomplished painters in the Arab world. Wife of a Lebanese doctor, she has a big, appreciative audience.

BUSY FABRICATORS *of films and television shows command an avid audience*

BRILLIANT DIRECTOR of Egyptian films, Yusif Shaheen stares intently at scenes from a new picture. Farmers and townsmen are equally enthusiastic movie-goers.

PLEADING LAWYER holds stage center in a drama produced by one of Cairo's two television stations, which carry educational programs in addition to entertainment.

*STUDENTS crowd
the universities
and the expanding
schools as the desire
for learning grows*

OFF TO SCHOOL, crisply dressed and bright-eyed children wait for their bus in Alexandria. If the present very rapid rate of school expansion continues, all Egyptian children under 12 may be attending primary school by 1970.

IN CLASS at the ancient university of al Azhar *(left)*, students still sit on the floor of the mosque at their teacher's feet. Until this century the courses were mainly in Islamic law and religion. Now secular subjects are taught.

IN MEDITATION in the misty morning, a student sits by a statue on the handsome campus of the University of Cairo. More than 100,000 scholars study at this institution and Egypt's three other purely secular universities.

10

An Uncommitted Future

THE zodiac of Arab states girdles the middle of the world. Arab islands or Arab-controlled deserts separate Europe—and the U.S.S.R.—from tropical Africa; the Suez Canal remains the greatest single waterway between East and West. Arab airports are way stations between the compass points. The oil which most of the ships in the canal or the jets in the air depend on is likely to have come from the world through which they pass: minuscule Kuwait has proved oil reserves nearly as extensive as those of the entire Western Hemisphere. The ascending parabola of Arab development makes the Middle East market potentially one of the most attractive and profitable in the world.

The emergence of the United Nations as a world forum has given an influence to the 11 Arab member states greater than their voting power, for the Arabs now have alliances outside the confines of their world. New fuels, new routes and new markets have thus put the Arab lands back at the center of the world, where the medieval maps, with their fixation on the Holy Land, put them in the past.

Which way will the Arab states cast their votes, their influence and their friendship? At one time in recent history, it was widely suggested that Arab arms deals with the Russian bloc and Arab commercial arrangements with Communist countries were the first steps toward an acceptance of Communism. The 1957 Eisenhower Doctrine was formulated by the late John Foster Dulles with this fear in mind. But recent history has belied Dulles' apprehension. No Arab country tolerates a genuine Communist party. Tunisia allows a phantom organization to function, under strict surveillance, since President Habib Bourguiba's Neo-Destour party has such control over the country's political life that the Communists offer no more danger than the sham democratic parties do in Communist eastern Europe. In Iraq the government of Premier Abdul Karim Kassem has legalized not the genuine Communist party but a heretical group which is under Kassem's control. In Egypt, despite Soviet aid in building the Aswan High Dam, the few Communists that exist are kept under severe supervision. The same is true in other Arab countries.

COMMUNISM has failed to win Arab support for three reasons. The first is that the Arabs are essentially a religious people. Islam plays a more potent role in Arab countries than any form of Christianity does in the West, except perhaps in Roman Catholic Ireland. In Iraq—where for a time Communism seemed most dangerous—the mosque was the rallying point for national resistance. Secondly, Arabs are aware that Communist parties everywhere work for Russia. The Arab man in the street is far better informed than his sometimes tattered appearance might suggest. He listens selectively to the radios whose waves compete over his country. Jealous of his newly won independence after having so recently escaped from the British or the French, he has no wish to enter the Soviet empire; the significance of what happened in Hungary and Tibet is not lost on him.

Thirdly, despite their poetry, Arabs are realists. Many students and technicians have visited Communist countries. They return impressed by certain achievements, but at the same time repelled by the low standard of living and the lack of personal freedom. After the 1958 Iraqi revolution, hundreds of Iraqi students were sent to schools in Russia, Bulgaria and other eastern countries. Shortly afterward, the Communist-leaning Iraqi minister of education suggested to the students' families that their sons were doing the equivalent of military service and should not expect in Sofia or Moscow the luxuries to which they had been accustomed in Baghdad. Coming from a leftist in poverty-stricken Iraq, this was a surprising admission. Egyptians tell, too, of the times they have been accosted in Moscow and asked to part with their shoes for the black market.

Despite this aversion toward Communism, the Arab states have recently had hard words for the West. Part of this is caused by the memory of colonialism. Part comes from the Arabs' belief that some of their governments are kept in office only by the support of foreign powers. Part is resentment at the continued British control over Aden and Britain's protectorates on the Persian Gulf and the coast of southern Arabia. Part is the recent and bitter experience of warfare between Arabs and Frenchmen in Algeria. The French, as members of the North Atlantic Treaty Organization, were identified in Arab eyes with the whole of the West; some of the arms they used came from the United States. And although 1962 saw a general endorsement by the French in metropolitan France of the principle of Algerian self-determination, the rightist Secret Army Organization committed atrocities deliberately designed to inflame Moslems against Europeans in an attempt to prevent the achievement of independence.

BUT, in the opinion of the Arabs, the greatest obstacle to good relations between the West and the Arab world lies in the existence of Israel—a state for whose birth in their midst the Arabs blame England, France and the United States. The dispute between Israelis and Arabs also constitutes a major danger to world peace.

In his pessimistic novel *On the Beach*, the British writer Nevil Shute predicted an atomic war, accidentally started after a collision between Israel and the Arabs. Such a beginning to a world war, it could be argued, is as likely as one developing from a head-to-head impasse over Berlin. For an Arab-Israeli flare-up could conceivably involve the big powers, despite the implications of such involvement.

To the Arabs, the establishment of Israel in 1948 meant the physical loss of one fertile island in their archipelago. Until that time, the Zionist settlers had acquired by purchase only about 6 per cent of the land which was to constitute their new state. And, as it finally came into being, the new state was more than a third larger than it had been under the partition plan voted in 1947 by the United Nations, thanks to the victories and the territory won by Israel in the Arab-Israeli war. Today more than a million Arabs are refugees from Palestine; many have been born in the camps which dismally encircle Israel in Jordan, Syria and the Gaza Strip. They cannot be expected to forget their ancestral earth in a lifetime.

SOME 650,000 of these refugees originally left their homes because they were terrorized by a mounting campaign of violence. They did not abandon their rights any more than Frenchmen who moved south from Paris in flight from the Nazis in 1940 abandoned their rights to Parisian property. The U.N. has repeatedly asserted the right of the refugees to return or to be given compensation; yet Israel has categorically refused repatriation.

The Arabs' unwillingness to accept a *de facto* loss of territory and rights means that they refuse to accept Israel in its present form. Because they will not recognize its existence, Israel to them is a physical wall in the midst of their world: an Iraqi cannot motor overland to Cairo, and Egyptian cotton cannot be trucked to Lebanon. When Arabs are accused of being intransigent and aggressive, they point out that Israel has been condemned five times by the U.N. Security Council for armed attacks on Arab countries. Israel, they note, has also been rebuked many times by the U.N.'s Mixed Armistice Commissions for infractions of the armistice agreement. No Arab state has been

similarly condemned. To this argument Israel replies that it has been compelled to send troops into Arab territories to clean out the home bases of the irregulars who have been sent raiding into Israel.

Much of the talk about Israel and the Arabs is recriminatory and backward-looking, since to look forward with clear sight is difficult. In Israel, there is an exaltation of the army as a character-building, citizen-forming machinery, which is paralleled in most Arab countries. Except for this tenuous and ironic link, there is little shared by the enemies. Trade is nonexistent. The Arabs' total boycott of Israel does not harm the Arabs: Beirut's post-1948 boom is largely due to the elimination of what is now the Israeli seaport of Haifa as a transit port for Arab countries. Thus there is no economic motive for good relations. Israel produces little that the Arabs need.

Yet the West has a duty to regard the Arab conflict with Israel soberly, for the West has great responsibilities as well as interests in the area. The West's reputation and western interests have suffered through past decisions made hastily for inadequate reasons; to maintain the interests and repair the reputation, the West must first understand the problem and then act impartially—not under the sway of pressure groups, but judging each issue on its merits.

ARABS believe that if the West argues that Israeli shipping should be allowed to go through the Suez Canal (despite Egypt's claim that it has a right to stop the ships, since it still considers itself at war with Israel), then the West should also insist that U.N. resolutions be observed concerning the right of the refugees either to return to their lands or to receive compensation for their loss (and such compensation should be made realistically, not on the basis of a 1948 evaluation in terms of an Israeli currency which has since undergone a 93 per cent devaluation). But so far, the United Nations has not even been able to obtain compliance by either the Arabs or the Israelis with that part of the 1947 U.N. resolution that calls for the internationalization of Jerusalem.

As to the basic Israeli-Arab problem itself, time may perhaps ease the way for solutions that seem incredible at the moment. The new Israelis may feel readier to become part of the Arab world; almost one third of Israel's population consists either of Jews who came from Arab countries or of Arabs (nearly a quarter of a million) who have stayed in the country. As the memory of Europe recedes, a new willingness to integrate in the Arab East may become part of the general mood in Israel.

IN the Arab world itself, there has never been any racial feeling about Jews. As one Egyptian wryly put it when synagogues elsewhere were being daubed with swastikas, "The one country where Judaism is assured of tolerance is Egypt." This was not an empty boast. The attitude is in large measure due to the religious affinities between Judaism and Islam. Similar cultural affinities link the Arabs with the West; Arab value judgments are intelligible to the West, and vice versa. In a large sense, Arab civilization is part of western, not eastern, culture.

But the Arabs do not believe that the West has been impartial since the creation of Israel. Not surprisingly, they have sought friends elsewhere. Nasser long ago came to the conclusion that Egypt lay at the center of three circles of potential alliance: the Arab world, Islam and Africa. The Arabs as a whole have now discovered fruitful relationships south of the Sahara and in Asia. With the discovery of these friendships has come, too, the discovery of nonalignment. On one level, this policy may be viewed as the egoism of neutrality coupled with an opportunism that seeks aid from both sides by a blackmail process. But to accept such a diagnosis as complete would be wrong.

In the first place, nonalignment is not a crafty slogan thought up by politicians. It is an attitude with great appeal throughout Africa and Asia. Observers agree that Nasser did not enjoy widespread popularity inside the Arab world until he returned from the 1955 Bandung Conference in Indonesia, where a wide spectrum of African and Asian countries formulated what came to be known as "positive neutralism." Pro-western Arabs are nearly always those who for one reason or another are distrusted by their own peoples, just as pro-Soviet Arabs are similarly distrusted. For centuries the darker races have been pawns in other men's games. The Africans and Asians, bitterly aware of the extent to which they lag behind western standards of living, want to build, and build quickly, and not be involved in wars whose causes seem remote.

In the second place, idealists in Africa and Asia believe that by pursuing a policy of nonalignment they are helping a bigger cause than their own. Admittedly, there is often an aroma of smugness and self-satisfaction to their arguments; they sometimes seem more ready to criticize the West (which has freed its colonies) than the East (which has not). Yet ideologically they are often clear-cut in their opposition to Communism. Nasser, for example, has stated his opposition repeatedly.

IT can be argued that the existence of a large bloc of nonaligned states does have the tempering effect of leading both sides in the cold war to measure their words and bring their actions into line with them. In the way they have voted on crucial issues, the Afro-Asian countries have surprised those who assumed they would act in herdlike unison. On the contrary, the nonaligned states have assessed most problems individually and voted accordingly.

The 80 million Arabs, for all that makes them exotic, attractive or maddening to outsiders, are men and women working out problems in an area whose importance to them is neither strategic nor political, but domestic. To themselves, in their demand to be understood by an outside world which they seldom try to understand themselves, they are not intransigent—they are merely like everyman whose ego forms the center of his world. Yet the Arabs are, in the words of Gamal Abdul Nasser, "a sentimental people. A kind word means more to them than a million dollars." In this regard they are once again like people everywhere.

New apartments for industrial workers rise outside Aswan. Next page: Arabs pause by the great, crenelated walls in the city of Fez.

DETERMINED to win themselves full partnership in the modern world . . .

. . . the Arab peoples also wish to preserve their rich heritage of art and wisdom,

their vigorous faith, their sense of a cultural solidarity that links each to all

Appendix

HISTORICAL DATES

B.C.

c.4000 Beginnings of settlement in what is to become the Arab heartland—the Tigris-Euphrates Valley and along the Nile

c.750-275 Assyrian, Persian and Greek empires successively engulf the Middle East

64 Rome begins to divide the area into provinces

A.D.

305 Control of the Middle East passes to Byzantium

c.570 Mohammed born in Mecca

610 Mohammed begins to win converts to the new religion called Islam

622 Mohammed and his converts move to Medina to escape persecution and organize a religious community. The migration marks the beginning of the Islamic era

630 Mohammed returns to Mecca in triumph

632 Death of Mohammed. His father-in-law, Abu Bakr, is chosen as the first caliph

633-644 Converts sweep out of the Arabian deserts and conquer Byzantine, Persian and North African territories

655-661 Civil war develops over the succession to the caliphate. After the murder of Ali, son-in-law of Mohammed, Muawiya, a member of the Umayya family of Mecca, attains the office, despite opposition from Ali's followers, known as Shiites

661 Damascus becomes the Umayyad capital

670-699 Umayyads conquer parts of Tunisia, Algeria and Morocco

681 A band of Ali's partisans is massacred by Umayyads. Advocating vengeance, the Shiite group develops into a major religious movement in opposition to the Sunnite (orthodox) body

711 Moslems invade Spain

732 Moslem expansion into western Europe halted at the Battle of Tours in France

750 Dissension bred by Umayyad decadence and Shiites' growing strength leads to the overthrow of the dynasty. Abu al Abbas, a descendant of Mohammed's uncle, founds the Abbasid line

756 Prince Abdul Rahman establishes an independent dynasty in Spain

762 Abbasids found a capital at Baghdad which acquires fame as an intellectual center

788-800 Separatist movements begun in Spain spread to North Africa. Local dynasties are established first in Morocco, then in Tunisia

868 Ahmed ibn Tulun, a military leader and former Turkish slave, leads a revolt in Egypt, later extends his dominion to Syria

910 Obaidallah, who claims descent from Mohammed's daughter, Fatima, comes to power in Tunisia and founds the Fatimid line

969 Fatimids conquer Egypt, found Cairo and make it their capital

1070-1080 Seljuk Turks, converts to Islam who infiltrate the Arab empire from central Asia, defeat the Byzantines in Asia Minor, move on to Syria and Palestine

1096-1099 Crusaders arrive in the Middle East, conquer Jerusalem and gradually build a chain of feudal principalities along the eastern Mediterranean coast

1171 Saladin, a Kurdish army officer, deposes Fatimids, founds a Sunnite dynasty in Egypt and Syria

1187 Saladin defeats the Crusaders near Jerusalem

1221 Mongol troops of Genghis Khan overrun eastern regions of the Moslem world

1250 The first Mameluke (slave) sultan comes to power in Egypt. Mamelukes are to rule Egypt and Syria for 250 years

1258-1260 Mongols capture Baghdad, toppling the long-weak Abbasid caliphate, but are finally checked in Palestine by Egypt's armies

1260 A dispossessed Abbasid heir is installed as a puppet caliph in Cairo under the Mamelukes

c.1300 Uthman, or Osman, an ambitious military leader after whom the Ottoman, or Osmanli, Empire is named, begins a series of conquests in western Turkey

1400 Attacks by forces of Timur the Lame (Tamerlane), restorer of Genghis Khan's Mongol empire, devastate Iraq and Syria

1453 Constantinople falls to Islam under attack of the Ottoman sultan Mehmed II

1492 Christians conquer Granada, last Moslem stronghold in Spain

1516-1517 Ottomans take Syria and Egypt, hang the last Mameluke sultan and remove the puppet caliph to Constantinople

1639 Ottomans take Iraq from Persia

c.1750 Mohammed ibn Abdul Wahhab launches a fundamentalist reform campaign in central Arabia

1798-1801 Napoleon invades Egypt, later is expelled by the British and Turks

1830-1849 France conquers Algeria

1832-1882 Egypt gains semi-independence from Ottomans

1861 European powers force Ottomans to recognize an autonomous Lebanon

1869 Completion of Suez Canal

1881-1883 France conquers Tunisia, British occupy Egypt

1898 Sir Horatio Kitchener leads an Anglo-Egyptian force into the Sudan and suppresses the Mahdist movement

1916-1924 Hussein ibn Ali of the Hashemite family of Mecca leads a revolt against the Turks in western Arabia, rules until he is overpowered by the Wahhabis under Abdul Aziz ibn Saud

1917 Britain issues the Balfour Declaration, favoring the establishment of a national home in Palestine for the Jews

1918 Turkey's defeat in World War I ends Ottoman rule in Arab lands. The empire is dissolved

1920 League of Nations gives mandates over Syria and Lebanon to France and mandates over Palestine, Transjordan and Iraq to Britain

1921-1932 Ibn Saud consolidates north and central Arabia into the kingdom of Saudi Arabia

1932-1946 As mandates end, Syria and Lebanon become republics. Hashemite heirs are enthroned—Feisal in Iraq and Abdullah in Transjordan

1936 Britain recognizes the independence of Egypt

1938 Oil in commercial quantities found in Saudi Arabia

1945 The Arab League organized

1948 The state of Israel is proclaimed after Britain's termination of its Palestine mandate. Brief war between Arab states and Israel is won by Israel

1951 Libya gains independence

1952 A military coup ousts King Farouk in Egypt

1954 Algeria revolts against French rule

1956 The Sudan, Tunisia and Morocco win independence. Gamal Abdul Nasser becomes president of Egypt. Britain, France and Israel invade Egypt after Nasser nationalizes the Suez Canal, later withdraw under U.N. pressure

1958 Egypt and Syria form the United Arab Republic. A military revolt overthrows the Iraqi monarchy

1961 Syria withdraws from the U.A.R.

FOR FURTHER READING

CHAPTER I: UNITY OF THE DISUNITED

Anshen, Ruth Nanda, *Mid-East: World-Center*. Harper & Brothers, 1956.

Atlas of the Arab World and the Middle East. St. Martin's Press, 1960.

Brockelmann, Carl, *History of the Islamic Peoples*. G. P. Putnam's Sons, 1960.

Coon, Carleton S., *Caravan: The Story of the Middle East*. Henry Holt, 1958.

Cressey, George B., *Crossroads: Land and Life in Southwest Asia*. J. B. Lippincott, 1960.

Faris, Nabih Amin, *The Arab Heritage*. Princeton University Press, 1946.

Fisher, Sydney Nettleton, *The Middle East: A History*. Alfred A. Knopf, 1959.

Fisher, W. B., *The Middle East: A Physical, Social and Regional Geography*. E.P. Dutton, 1961.

Hazard, Harry W., and H. Lester Cooke Jr., *Atlas of Islamic History*. Princeton University Press, 1954.

Hitti, Philip K., *History of the Arabs*. St. Martin's Press, 1960.

Kirk, George E., *A Short History of the Middle East*. Frederick A. Praeger, 1959.

The Middle East. Survey and directory. Europa Publications, London, 1961.

Yale, William, *The Near East: A Modern History*. University of Michigan Press, 1958.

CHAPTER II: CULTURE, PAST AND PRESENT

Ali, Abdullah Yusuf, *The Holy Quran*. Arabic text, translation and commentary. Hafner Publishing, 1946.

Antonius, George, *The Arab Awakening*. G. P. Putnam's Sons, 1946.

Arabian Nights. Viking Press, 1952.

Arnold, Sir Thomas, and Alfred Guillaume, *The Legacy of Islam*. Oxford University Press, 1931.

Creswell, K.A.C., *A Short Account of Muslim Architecture*. Penguin Books, 1958.

Dermenghem, Emile, *Muhammad and the Islamic Tradition*. Harper & Brothers, 1958.

Ettinghausen, Richard, *Arab Painting*. Albert Skira, Geneva, Switzerland, 1962.

Gibb, H.A.R., *Mohammedanism: An Historical Survey*. Oxford University Press, 1953.

Guillaume, Alfred, *The Life of Muhammad*. Oxford University Press, 1955.

Hitti, Philip K., *The Near East in History*. D. Van Nostrand, 1961.

Iqbal, Sir Mohammad, *The Reconstruction of Religious Thought in Islam*. Ashraf Press, Lahore, Pakistan, 1951.

Lewis, Bernard, *The Arabs in History*. Harper & Brothers, 1960.

Nicholson, R. A., *A Literary History of the Arabs*. Cambridge University Press, 1930.

Watt, W. Montgomery, *Muhammad at Mecca*. Oxford University Press, 1953.

Muhammad, Prophet and Statesman. Oxford University Press, 1961.

Young, T. Cuyler, *Near Eastern Culture and Society*. Princeton University Press, 1951.

CHAPTER III: THE COLONIAL ERA

DeGaury, Gerald, *Rulers of Mecca*. Roy Publishers, 1954.

Hitti, Philip K., *Lebanon in History*. St. Martin's Press, 1957.

Hurewitz, J. C., *Diplomacy in the Near and Middle East*. D. Van Nostrand, 1956. *Middle East Dilemmas*. Harper & Brothers, 1953.

CHAPTER IV: LEVANTINES AND ZEALOTS

Doughty, Charles M., *Travels in Arabia Deserta*. Doubleday, 1955.

Evans-Pritchard, E. E., *The Sanusi of Cyrenaica*. Oxford University Press, 1949.

Philby, H. St. John, *Arabia of the Wahhabis*. Constable and Co., London, 1928.

The Middle East: A Political and Economic Survey. Oxford University Press, 1958.

Thesiger, Wilfred, *Arabian Sands*. E. P. Dutton, 1959.

Ziadeh, N. A., *Syria and Lebanon*. Frederick A. Praeger, 1957.

CHAPTER V: THE VILLAGE

Ammar, Hamed, *Growing Up in an Egyptian Village*. Routledge & Kegan Paul, Ltd., London, 1954.

Ayrout, Father Henry, *The Fellaheen*. Les Editions Universitaires, Cairo, Egypt, 1947.

Sharkawi, A. R. *Egyptian Earth*. William Heinemann, Ltd., London, 1962.

Warriner, Doreen, *Land Reform and Development in the Middle East*. Oxford University Press, 1957.

CHAPTER VI: OIL AND WATER

Atiyah, Edward, *The Arabs*. Penguin Books, 1955.

Dickson, H.R.P., *The Arab of the Desert*. George Allen and Unwin, London, 1951.

Lenczowski, George, *Oil and State in the Middle East*. Cornell University Press, 1960.

Longrigg, Stephen Hemsley, *Oil in the Middle East*. Oxford University Press, 1954.

Philby, H. St. John, *Saudi Arabia*. Frederick A. Praeger, 1955.

Sanger, Richard H., *The Arabian Peninsula*. Cornell University Press, 1951.

Shwadran, Benjamin, *The Middle East: Oil and the Great Powers*. Frederick A. Praeger, 1955.

Van Der Meulen, D., *The Wells of Ibn Saud*. Frederick A. Praeger, 1957.

CHAPTER VII: EGYPT AND NASSER

Ahmed, Jamal, *Intellectual Origins of Egyptian Nationalism*. Oxford University Press, 1960.

Berger, Morroe, *Bureaucracy and Society in Modern Egypt*. Princeton University Press, 1957.

Issawi, Charles, *Egypt at Mid-Century: An Economic Survey*. Oxford University Press, 1954.

Lacouture, Jean and Simonne, *Egypt in Transition*. Criterion Books, 1958.

Little, Tom, *Egypt*. Frederick A. Praeger, 1958.

Nasser, Gamal Abdul, *Egypt's Liberation: The Philosophy of the Revolution*. Public Affairs Press, 1955.

Sadat, Anwar El, *Revolt on the Nile*. John Day, 1957.

St. John, Robert, *The Boss*. McGraw-Hill, 1960.

Stewart, Desmond, *Young Egypt*. Wingate, London, 1958.

Wheelock, Keith, *Nasser's New Egypt*. Frederick A. Praeger, 1960.

Wynn, Wilton, *Nasser of Egypt*. Arlington Books, 1959.

CHAPTER VIII: ARAB NATIONALISM

Ashford, Douglas E., *Political Change in Morocco*. Princeton University Press, 1961.

Barbour, Nevill, *Survey of North West Africa*. Oxford University Press, 1959.

Gillespie, Joan, *Algeria: Rebellion and Revolution*. Frederick A. Praeger, 1960.

Jarvis, H. Wood, *Pharaoh to Farouk*. Macmillan, 1956.

Landau, Rom, *Morocco Independent*. George Allen and Unwin, London, 1961.

Marlowe, John, *Arab Nationalism and British Imperialism*. Frederick A. Praeger, 1961.

Morris, James, *Hashemite Kings*. Pantheon, 1959. *Sultan in Oman*. Pantheon, 1957.

Villard, Henry Serrano, *Libya, the New Arab Kingdom of North Africa*. Cornell University Press, 1956.

CHAPTER X: THE FUTURE

Berger, Morroe, *The Arab World Today*. Doubleday, 1962.

Fernau, Friedrich W., *Moslems on the March*. Alfred A. Knopf, 1954.

Kritzeck, James, and R. Bayly Winder, *The World of Islam*. St. Martin's Press, 1960.

Mechin, Jacques B., *Arabian Destiny*. Essential Books, 1958.

Morris, James, *Islam Inflamed*. Pantheon, 1957.

Peretz, Don, *Israel and the Palestine Arabs*. Middle East Institute, 1958.

FAMOUS FIGURES AND WORKS IN ARAB CULTURE

LITERATURE

Imru al Qays
Tarafa ibn al Abd
Amr ibn Kulthum
Harith ibn Halliza   } Before 622 A.D.   Pre-Islamic poets whose works are collected in the *Muallaqat (Suspended Odes)*
Antara ibn Shaddad
Zuhayr ibn Abi Sulma
Labid ibn Rabia

Jarir	?-c.729	Poetical satires and panegyrics
Ibn al Muqaffa	?-757	*Book of Kalila and Dimna*, stories derived from Sanskrit fables
Rabia al Adawiyya	c.717-c.801	First female Arab saint, wrote *Sufi* poetry
Abu Newas	?-810	Poems celebrating wine and women
Abu Tammam	?-845	*Hamasa (Fortitude)*, anthology of poems
al Jahiz	?-869	*Book of Animals*, zoological essay which contains much theology and folklore
Tabari	838-923	*Annals of the Apostles and the Kings*, collection of original historical documents
al Kindi	c.850-?	Earliest of prominent philosophers, also famed as an astronomer, mathematician and music theorist
	10th Century	*Alf Laylah wa Laylah (The Thousand and One Nights)*, tales from an older Persian collection adapted to the time of Haroun al Rashid and later caliphs
Ibn Abd Rabbihi	?-940	*The Unique Necklace*, by the first great Arab poet of Spain
al Farabi	?-950	Essays on philosophy, politics, psychology and music theory
Mutanabbi	915-965	*Diwan*, collection of poems
Faraj al Isfahani	c.897-967	Twenty-volume *Book of Songs*
al Maarri	973-1057	*Luzumiyyat*, philosophy reflecting skepticism of the era
Ali ibn Hazm	994-1064	*The Book of Religion and Sects*, also an anthology of love verse, *The Ring of the Dove*
Ghazali	1058-1111	*Revivification of the Religious Sciences* and *Collapse of the Philosophers*, theological essays
Ibn Tufayl	?-1185	*Alive, Son of Awake*, allegorical novel
Ibn Rushd (Averroes)	1126-1198	Commentaries on works of Aristotle and numerous other contributions in philosophy, medicine, mathematics and law
Ibn Arabi	1165-1240	*Meccan Revelations* and *Bezels of Philosophy*, treatises on mysticism
Ibn Khaldun	1332-1406	Histories and philosophies of the development of civilization, including *Book of Examples*
Ahmed Showky	1868-1932	Egyptian. Poems: *Al Showkiyat*. Novels: *Maid of India*. Plays
Hafiz Ibrahim	1871-1932	Egyptian. Novels: *Nights of Satih*. Poems
Maruf al Rasafi	1875-1945	Iraqi. Poems: *Diwan al Rasafi*
Bishara al Khouri	1882-	Lebanese. Poems: *Al Hawa wa Shabab*
Kahlil Gibran	1883-1931	Lebanese-American. Poems: *The Prophet*
Taha Hussein	1889-	Egyptian. Novels: *The Days*. Translations of Sophocles and Shakespeare into Arabic prose
Ilia Abu Madi	1890-1957	Lebanese-American. Poems: *Al Jadawil (The Flowing Brook)* and *Al Khamael (The Prairie)*
Mahmoud Teymour	1894-	Egyptian. Short stories: *Tales from Egyptian Life*. Novels and plays
Towfik al Hakim	1902-	Egyptian. Novels: *Sparrow from the East*. Plays: *People of the Cave*
Naguib Mahfouz	1916-	Egyptian. Novels: *A Narrow Lane* and *Khan al Khalili*

PAINTING AND SCULPTURE

Mahmoud Said	1897-	Egyptian. Paintings: *Shadoofs at Work* and *The Donkey*
Hamed Abdalla	1917-	Egyptian. Paintings: *Where Are They Going?* Crystal engravings: *The Lovers*
Jewad Saleem	1920-1961	Iraqi. Sculpture: Monument in Baghdad commemorating the 1958 revolution. Paintings
Aida Marini	1925-	Lebanese. Paintings: *Sunset, Redemption* and *Hopscotch*
Tahia Halim	1926-	Egyptian. Paintings: *Hurgada* and *The Red Sea*

SCIENCE

Jabir ibn Hayyan (Geber)	?-790	Alchemy. Treatise on pharmacology
al Kwarizimi	780-c.850	Mathematics. Invented modern algebra and introduced the Arabic numerals called algorisms
al Battani	858-929	Astronomy. Proved the possibility of annular eclipses of the sun
al Razi	865-925	Medicine and chemistry. Wrote a medical encyclopedia, a treatise on smallpox and the *Book of Secrets*, for centuries the primary chemistry source
al Masudi	912-956	Geography. Thirty-volume encyclopedia
al Majusi (Haly Abbas)	?-944	Wrote on childbirth and capillary system
Ibn al Haytham (Alhazen)	965-1039	Physics. Treatises *On Optics* and *On Light*
al Biruni	973-1048	Mathematics. Perfected a method for determining latitude and longitude, discussed possibility of earth's rotation on its axis
Ibn Sina (Avicenna)	980-1037	Medicine. Wrote *Book of Healing*. Also renowned as a philosopher
al Zarkali (Arzachel)	?-c.1087	Astronomy. Wrote a treatise, later used by Copernicus, on an astrolabe he invented
Ibn Zuhr (Avenzoar)	c.1091-1162	Medicine. Works on therapeutics and diet
Ibn Battutah	1304-1377	Geography. Accounts of his travels to central Africa, India and China
Salah Hadayat	1920-	Nuclear physics. Egyptian minister for scientific research

Dome of the Rock	c.688-692	Jerusalem. Built on traditional site of Abraham's sacrifice where Solomon's Temple later stood. Design was derived from the shrine over the tomb of Christ
Great Mosque of Qairawan	Late 7th-early 13th Century	Tunisia. First of North African congregational mosques
Great Mosque of Damascus	c.706-715	Syria. Established the plan for all later congregational mosques
Great Mosque of Cordova	785-987	Spain. Despite 16th Century additions, finest surviving work of Umayyad architecture
Great Mosque of Samarra	Begun 847	Iraq. Built of brick in traditional Mesopotamian style. Its spiral minaret suggests a ziggurat
Mosque of Ibn Tulun	Completed 879	Cairo. Continued architectural tradition of Samarra in Egypt
Mosque of al Azhar	970 and later	Cairo. Now the nucleus of the oldest university of Islam
Alhambra Palace	c.1333-1391	Granada. Ultimate refinement of Umayyad style. Palace of the last Islamic rulers in Spain
Madrasa of Sultan Hassan	1356-1363	Cairo. Most outstanding cross-shaped mosque school. Design based on Persian prototypes
Tomb-mosque of Sultan Qayt Bay	1472-1474	Cairo. Finest of Mameluke monuments from last great period of Egyptian-Islamic architecture

POLITICAL UNITS IN THE ARAB WORLD

NAME	POP.	AREA (sq. mi.)	CAPITAL	GOVERNMENT
Aden (colony)	155,000	110	Aden	British Crown colony since 1937
Aden (protectorate)	660,000	112,000		Sheikdoms which became protectorates of Great Britain between 1886 and 1914
Algeria	11,020,000	919,590	Algiers	Became a French possession after 1830, achieved independence in 1962
Bahrain	147,000	231	Manama	Independent British-protected sheikdom
Iraq	7,085,000	171,599	Baghdad	Under British mandate until 1932, became a republic after the overthrow of the monarchy in 1958
Jordan	1,695,000	37,300	Amman	Under British mandate until 1946, now a monarchy
Kuwait	332,000	6,000	Kuwait	Sheikdom, under British protection since 1899, acquired independence in 1961
Lebanon	1,646,000	4,015	Beirut	Under French mandate until 1943, now a republic
Libya	1,195,000	679,358	Tripoli and Bengasi	Italian colony until World War II, a monarchy since 1951
Morocco	11,626,000	171,305	Rabat	Spanish and French protectorate until 1956, now a monarchy
Muscat and Oman	550,000	82,000	Muscat	Independent British-protected sultanate
Qatar	40,000	8,500	Doha	Independent British-protected sheikdom
Saudi Arabia	6,036,000	617,760	Riyadh and Mecca	Monarchy
Syria	4,555,000	71,227	Damascus	Under French mandate until 1943, now a republic
The Sudan	12,109,000	967,498	Khartoum	Under British-Egyptian administration until 1956, now a republic
Trucial Oman (or States)	86,000	32,278		Seven independent British-protected sheikdoms
Tunisia	4,168,000	48,332	Tunis	French protectorate until 1956, now a republic
U.A.R. (Egypt)	27,000,000	386,100	Cairo	Monarchy until 1953, now a republic
Yemen	4,500,000	75,290	Sana	Monarchy

Credits

The sources for the illustrations in this book are shown below. Credits for pictures from left to right are separated by commas, top to bottom by dashes.

Cover: Joseph Nettis
8—Brassaï from Rapho-Guillumette
10—Map by Bill Dove
15, 16, 17—Joseph Nettis
18, 19—Emil Schulthess from Black Star, Sir Julian Huxley
20, 21—Brian Brake from Magnum, John Lewis Stage from Lensgroup, Lee Lockwood from Black Star
22, 23, 24—Joseph Nettis
27—Map by Bill Dove
31—The Metropolitan Museum of Art, Rogers Fund 1955
33—Bruce Conde
34, 35—John Lewis Stage from Lensgroup except left Larry Burrows
36—Salahuddin Khursheed
37—Mohamed Youssef from Akbar El Yom
38, 39—Desmond Stewart—Khamis Abdel Latif, Joseph Nettis
40—Bob Landry
49—Copy by Brian Seed
50—John Phillips
51—George Rodger—James Whitmore
52, 53—Left Howard Sochurek center; Larry Burrows right; James Burke
54, 55—Larry Burrows except bottom right United Press International
56—J. F. Tourtet
57—Burt Glinn from Magnum
58, 59—James Burke
62, 63—Courtesy the Misses S. D. and F. G. Doughty and Jonathan Cape Limited
65—Michael Rougier
66, 67—Elliott Erwitt from Magnum
68—Michael Rougier
69—James Burke
70, 71—George Rodger from Magnum except top left Samy H. Abboud and Khalil A. Nasr
72—Joseph Nettis

75—Elliott Erwitt from Magnum
79—Joseph Nettis
80—Metcalf from Black Star
81, 82, 83—Joseph Nettis
84—Pierre Boulat for TIME
87—Chart by Bill Dove
88—Map by Bill Dove
91—David Douglas Duncan
92—Hans Hubmann from Black Star
93—Joseph McKeown
94, 95—Dante Vacchi, John Lewis Stage from Lensgroup
96—Joseph Nettis
104—Joseph Nettis
105, 106, 107—James Burke
108—Eliot Elisofon
109—James Burke
110, 111—John Phillips—AFP from Pictorial Parade, Henri Cartier-Bresson from Magnum
112—Hassan Diab
113—Howard Sochurek
114, 115—Gordon Tenney
121—Camera Press from Pix
122—Sheldon Machlin
123—James Whitmore except top right Howard Sochurek
124—AFP from Pictorial Parade, Loomis Dean
125—Loomis Dean
126—Photo Researchers, Inc.
127—Frank J. Scherschel—Pierre Boulat
128, 129—Joseph Nettis
131—Nagi of Sabah El Kheir
136—Bernard Rouget from Rapho-Guillumette
137—Picture Post from Pix—Henri Cartier-Bresson from Magnum
138, 139—John Phillips, Elliott Erwitt from Magnum, Ben Schultz
140, 141—Khamis Abdel Latif
142—Joseph Nettis—Henri Cartier-Bresson from Magnum
143, 144—Joseph Nettis
149—Joseph Nettis
150, 151—Brassaï from Rapho-Guillumette

ACKNOWLEDGMENTS

The editors of this book are indebted to R. Bayly Winder, Associate Professor of Arabic Studies, Department of Oriental Studies, Princeton University, and to J. C. Hurewitz, Professor of Government, School of International Affairs, Columbia University. Both read and commented in detail on portions of the text.

Index

This symbol in front of a page number indicates a photograph or painting of the subject mentioned.

Production staff for Time Incorporated

Arthur R. Murphy Jr. (Vice President and Director of Production)

Robert E. Foy, James P. Menton and Caroline Ferri

Text photocomposed on Photon equipment

under the direction of Albert J. Dunn and Arthur J. Dunn

X

Printed by R. R. Donnelley & Sons Company, Crawfordsville, Indiana,

and The Safran Printing Company, Detroit, Michigan

Bound by R. R. Donnelley & Sons Company, Crawfordsville, Indiana

Paper by The Mead Corporation, Dayton, Ohio

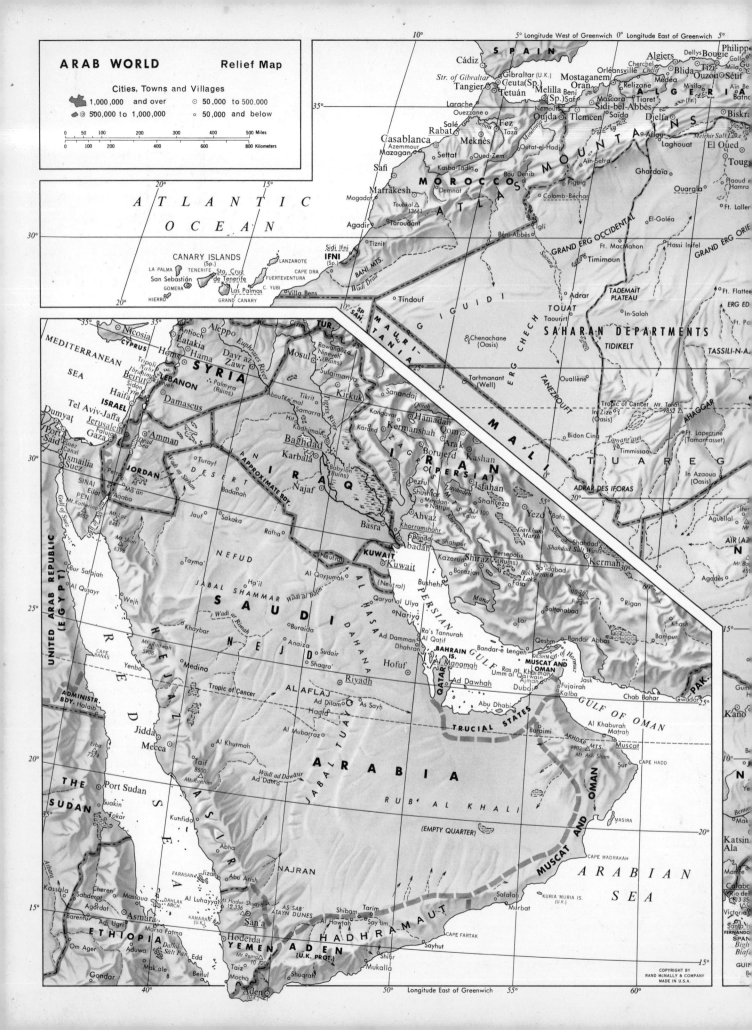

ARAB WORLD   Relief Map

Cities, Towns and Villages

- 1,000,000 and over
- 500,000 to 1,000,000
- ⊙ 50,000 to 500,000
- ○ 50,000 and below

0 50 100   200   300   400   500 Miles
0   100   200   400   600   800 Kilometers

5° Longitude West of Greenwich   0°   Longitude East of Greenwich   5°

SPAIN
Cádiz
Str. of Gibraltar
Tangier Gibraltar (U.K.)
Ceuta (Sp.)
Tetuán Melilla (Sp.)
Larache Beni
(Sp.) Saf
Salé Schott
Rabat Fez Taza
Meknès
Casablanca
Azemmour
Mazagan Oued-Zem
Outat-el-Hadj
Settat Kasba-Tadla
Safi Demnat
Bou Denib
Marrakesh Figuig
Mogador Toubkal △ 13661
Agadir Taroudant
Tiznit
Sidi Ifni BANI MTS.
IFNI (Sp.) Wadi Drâa
CAPE DRA

Algiers Dellys Bougie
Orléansville Cherchel Blida Philippe
Mostaganem Medea Sétif Golf
Relizane Misila
Oran Mascara Mila ALGERIA
Sidi-bel-Abbès (Fr.)
Oujda Tlemcen Saïda Djelfa
Nemours Aflou Melrhir Salt Lake
Aïn-Sefra Laghouat El Oued
Colomb-Béchar Ghardaïa Toug
Igli GRAND ERG OCCIDENTAL
Béni-Abbès Ouargla
GRAND ERG ORIE
Hassi Inifel
El-Goléa Ft. Flatte
Ft. MacMahon Haoud
Timimoun ERG ORIE
TADEMAÏT PLATEAU
In-Salah TIDIKELT
SAHARAN DEPARTMENTS
Chenachane (Oasis) Ft. Flatte
Ouallène ERG
Tropic of Cancer Mt. Tahat
In Zize (Oasis) 9852 △
Bidon Cinq Ft. Laperrine
(Tamanrasset)
Tamanrasset
In Azaoua (Oasis)
AHAGGAR
TUAREG
TASSILI-N-A
AÏR
Iferé
Aguella
Agadès
N

ATLANTIC
OCEAN

CANARY ISLANDS (Sp.)
LA PALMA Sta. Cruz de Tenerife
TENERIFE LANZAROTE
San Sebastián CAPE DRA
GOMERA FUERTEVENTURA
HIERRO C. YUBI
Las Palmas
GRAND CANARY
Villa Bens

SP. SAH.
MAURITANIA
IGUIDI
ERG CHECH
TANEZROUFT
ADRAR DES IFORAS
MALI

Nicosia
CYPRUS
MEDITERRANEAN SEA
Antioch Aleppo TUR.
Latakia Euphrates River Rawanduz
Tripoli Homs Hama Nineveh (Ruins) Ninevé
Nahr Dayr az Zawr Mosul
Beirut Ibrahim Sulaimanya
LEBANON SYRIA Sanandaj
Sidon Palmyra (Ruins) Kirkuk
Tyre Abou Kemal Qush
Damascus Tikrit Kangavar Hamadan
Haifa Samarra Karand Qom
Tel Aviv-Jaffa Kadhimain Kermanshah
ISRAEL Hit Baghdad Borujerd Arak
Dumyat Jerusalem Amman Karbala Babylon Kashan
Gaza Dead (Ruins) Dezful Isfahan
Port Said Sea Turayf Najaf Shushtar Shahreza
Suez Canal JORDAN Wadi as Sirhan IRAQ Meydan-e Naftun Yezd
Ismailia Ma'an DESERT APPROXIMATE BDY. Ahvaz Bafq
Suez Petra Badanah Lavandeh
SINAI PEN. Aqaba Jauf Sakaka Khorramshahr Kazerun Shiraz Sa'idabad
Mt. Katherine Rafha Abadan Bandar-e Persepolis Shahdad
8652 Mt. Loz Shapur (Ruins) Kermah
Bur Safajah 8461 Neutral KUWAIT Bushehr Borazjan
Al Qusair Mt. Sharr Tayma NEFUD Al Qaysumah Kuwait Lar
6398 Ha'il (Neutral)
Wejh JABAL SHAMMAR Wadi al Batin Qaryat al Ulya
CAPE BANAS Khaybar SAUDI Nariya Soltanabad
Mt. Radwah Buraida Ad Damman Al Qatif Rigan
5906 Wadi ar Rimah NEJD Sudair Dhahran Bandar Abbas
Yenbo Anaiza Shaqra Hofuf BAHRAIN IS. Qeshm Khash
Medina DAHANA Al Manamah Bampur
AL HASA MUSCAT AND OMAN
Tropic of Cancer Riyadh QATAR Ras al Khaima
AL AFLAJ Ad Dawhah Umm al Ajman Jask
Jidda Ad Dilam As Sayh Dubai Kalba Chab Bahar
Erba JABAL TUWAYQ Hariq Abu Dhabi Gwadar
7574 Mecca Al Mubarraz TRUCIAL STATES PAK.
Mt. Ibrahim Buraimi Al Khaburah GULF OF OMAN Gwadar
Taif Wadi ad Dawasir Matrah Kano
8500 Ad Dam ARABIA AKHDAR MTS. Muscat
THE Port Sudan ASIR 9902 Mt. Ash Sham Sur CAPE HADD
SUDAN Suakin RUB' AL KHALI
Tokar Kunfida (EMPTY QUARTER) MASIRA
Abha MUSCAT AND OMAN Katsin
ADMINISTR. BDY. Halaib Abu Arish NAJRAN CAPE MADRAKAH Ala
Erba Jizan ARABIAN SEA
Kassala DAHLAK ARCH. Al Luhayyah FARASAN Salalah
Cheren KAMARAN (U.K.) Mt. Hadur Shuayb AS SAB Shibam Tarim Murbat
Sabderat 12336 ATAYN DUNES Say'un KURIA MURIA IS. (U.K.)
Agordat San'a HADHRAMAUT CAPE FARTAK
ETHIOPIA Hodeida Mt. Rema YEMEN ADEN Sayhut
Marsa Fatma 10720 △ (U.K. PROT.) Shibr
Asmara Edd Taiz Mukalla
Barentu Dallol Salt Pan Al Haytam CAPE FARTAK
Adi Ugri Mocha Shuqrah
Om Ager Mak'ale Benul
Gondar Aden

RED SEA
HEJAZ
PERSIAN GULF
IRAN (PERSIA)
UNITED ARAB REPUBLIC (EGYPT)

COPYRIGHT BY
RAND McNALLY & COMPANY
MADE IN U.S.A.

Longitude East of Greenwich